11-18-73

To GEORG

with best wishes !

Harry & Burraghn

1

This book is dedicated to Don,
Lu, Anne Young and the
People of Alaska.

CONTENTS

FOREWORD: THE LAST FRONTIER

As someone who loves to travel, I will never forget the day I arrived at the Ted Stevens Anchorage International Airport and got my first glimpse of the spectacular scenery of the Chugach Mountains. Alaska is breathtakingly beautiful and one of the few places in the world I've visited that far exceeded expectations.

In the words of famous naturalist John Muir who traveled extensively throughout Alaska, "In the evening, after witnessing the unveiling of the majestic peaks and glaciers … it seems inconceivable that nature could have anything finer to show us. Nevertheless, compared with what was to come the next morning, all that was as nothing."

Alaska is the Aleut word for "Great Land." It is enormous with 586,412 square miles. By comparison, the state is 2 ½ times the size of Texas, 3 ½ times the size of California, and 488 times the size of our smallest state, Rhode Island. Alaska has 6,640 miles of coastline or more than the other 49 states combined. It has three million lakes, 29,000 square miles of glaciers, the largest mountain Kenai in North America, 20 official state languages, and one of the most productive fishing industries in the world. Alaska's state motto is "North to the Future" and its nickname is "The Last Frontier."

While Alaska has only been a state for 59 years, Aleut, Haida, and Tlingit people first settled it more than 20,000 years ago. These first Alaskans utilized the vast resources of fish, timber, and wildlife. Sadly, their peaceful lives were abruptly and dramatically changed with the unwanted arrival of Russian fur hunters. In an effort to expand his realm, Emperor Peter the Great commissioned Danish Captain Vitus Bering to explore eastward from Siberia's Kamchatka Peninsula. In 1741, Captain Bering spotted Mount St. Elias in southeastern Alaska and docked his ship *St. Gabriel* on Kayak Island. Within a few years, Russian hunters and traders were arriving in the Aleutian Islands.

Alaskan natives were forced to work for Russian fur hunters. It was their job to find, kill, and process sea otters in dangerous Alaskan waters. They were so successful that the Russian-American Company once sold 3,000 pelts for $150,000. This was an enormous amount of money. Sadly, Alaskan natives received a pittance for their hard work and any effort to end their enslavement was swiftly met with severe punishment and death. According to author John David Ragan, "Large numbers of Aleut men were shot and killed, and many Aleut women were raped or forced into concubines or 'marriage' with the Russians. The name given to the island's largest body of water Massacre Bay is grim commemoration of the slaughter that took place on Attu." It has been estimated that by 1791, Russians had annihilated two-thirds of the Aleut population through the introduction of foreign diseases, mistreatment, murder, and starvation.

Although the first Russian settlement was established at Three Saints Bay on Kodiak Island in 1784, Russia never intended to colonize what they called Russian America. At most, some 900 Russians lived in Alaska and by the 1860's the sea otter population had been decimated. With the loss of this valuable resource, Emperor Alexander II began to entertain the idea of selling Russian America to the United States. Russia had signed a treaty with the U.S. in 1824, which recognized their legal claim to the land. The Emperor's problem was that the bloody American Civil War had just ended, Congress had decided to impeach and remove President Andrew Johnson from office, and Alexander needed America to offer to buy this vast property.

Fortunately, Secretary of State William Seward was a willing partner who was deeply interested in enhancing his legacy by purchasing Alaska. In a speech, Secretary Seward had said, "Our population is destined to roll its resistless waves to the icy barriers of the North, and to encounter Oriental civilizations on the shores of the Pacific." In March 1867, Secretary Seward met with Russian Minister Edouard de Stoeckl. After difficult negotiations, the United States and Russia signed a treaty at 4:00 a. m. on

Saturday, March 30, 1867. The key terms of the treaty were a payment of $7.2 million to Russia and the stipulation that the land would convey to the United States prior to a Congressional appropriation.

Upon its signing, newspapers throughout the United States called the acquisition "Seward's Folly" or "Seward's Icebox." The *New York Evening Post* called the land, "Frozen, sterile region of no value." The *Chicago Republican* said, the purchase was, "A huge farce." As someone who had survived a brutal attack on April 15, 1865 by Lincoln's assassins, Secretary Seward was not dissuaded by newspaper editorials.

The United States Senate excised its constitutional responsibility by approving the Treaty of Cessation by a vote of 37 to 2 on April 9, 1867. President Johnson signed the treaty on May 28, 1867. The land was formally transferred in Sitka on October 18, 1867 when Russian Captain Alexis Peshchurov removed the Russian flag and Brigadier General Lovell H. Rousseau proudly replaced it with Old Glory.

Finally, a year later, the U.S. House of Representatives voted 113 to 44 to appropriate the $7.2 million. This was not the institutions finest hour. It was, however, a remarkable achievement for Secretary of State Seward and Russian Emperor Alexander II. Unlike Peter the Great, Alexander was not interested in expanding the Russian Empire. He was a pacifist who will be remembered for not only selling Alaska but also freeing all Russian serfs in 1861. By signing the Emancipation Edict, he earned the nickname of "Alexander the Liberator."

In 2017, Alaska celebrated the 150th Anniversary of the Treaty of Cessation. It is indisputable that the price of $7.2 million or two cents per acre was an incredible bargain. With the acquisition, the United States obtained vast amounts of coal, fish, oil, precious metals, timber, and wildlife. It is, therefore, not surprising that many historians now believe, "The Alaska Purchase was not Seward's Great Folly; it was his greatest achievement."

After being purchased from Russia, this vast addition to the United States was renamed Alaska. Between 1867 and 1959, it was governed by the federal government as the Department of Alaska, the District of Alaska, and the Territory of Alaska. Like most acquisitions, the U.S. Congress implemented various laws to manage and gradually allow local citizens a greater voice in determining their own future.

Among the most significant was the enactment of the Second Organic Act in April 1912. Under this law, Alaska became a U.S. territory with an elected legislature of eight Senators and 16 members of a House of Representatives. The territorial Governor remained an appointed position. Regrettably, all measures approved by the new territorial legislature were subject to

Congressional review. The federal government also retained the power to regulate fish, game, and fur resources. This was the first time a territory had been denied this responsibility and it violated the primacy clause of the U.S. Constitution that stipulates that the power to regulate fish and wildlife is retained by territories and states.

One of the first measures approved by the territorial legislature was to allow women the right to vote. This occurred in 1913 or seven years before the 19th Amendment to our constitution. This amendment states that, "The right of citizens of the United States to vote shall not be denied or abridged by the United States or by any state on account of sex." It took 42 years for the Congress and the states to approve this amendment. It took the Alaska legislature just one year to end this historic injustice.

In 1942, the Imperial Japanese Army bombed Dutch Harbor and occupied the Alaskan Aleutian Islands of Attu and Kiska. This was the only U.S. territory they controlled during World War II. As a result of this invasion, thousands of Americans were sent to Alaska to build and maintain military bases.

This also motivated the federal government to build a highway connecting the lower 48 states and Alaska across Canada. Under the leadership of the U.S. Army Corps of Engineers, 16,000 soldiers and civilians spent nine months constructing a 1,422-mile Alaskan highway. This highway, which cost $138 million, runs between Dawson Creek, British Columbia and Delta Junction, Alaska. It was a critical supply route. Its construction was also in the words of an Army Colonel the, "Biggest and hardest job since the Panama Canal."

In 1943, after 19 days of intense fighting including banzai charges, the U.S. Army's 7th Infantry Division crushed the Japanese invading forces. The Japanese lost 2,850 men and 29 surrendered. By contrast, the U.S. Army suffered 549 deaths and more than 1,000 wounded soldiers. For the rest of the war, over 150,000 U.S. troops were stationed in Alaska.

With the end of the war, Alaskan politicians such as E. L. "Bob" Bartlett, William A. Egan, Ernest Gruening, and Ted Stevens worked tirelessly for statehood. As an elected non-voting delegate to the House of Representatives from 1945 to 1959, Bob Bartlett, who is known as the architect of Alaskan Statehood, introduced statehood bills and worked to persuade his colleagues to support them.

In 1955, the Alaska Constitutional Convention met in Constitution Hall at the University of Alaska Fairbanks. There were 55 elected delegates at the Convention, which was the exact number that met at the Philadelphia Convention in 1787. The President of the Convention was Territorial Senator William A. Egan. For 73 days, the delegates worked to produce an Alaskan State Constitution. I am sure they were inspired by the words of Alexander Hamilton, Thomas Jefferson, and James Madison.

On April 11, 1955, former territorial Governor Gruening presented his views in a keynote speech entitled, "Let us end American Colonialism." A key passage was, "This Constitutional Convention is an important mobilization. But the battle still lies ahead, and it will require all our fortitude, audacity, resoluteness … and maybe some more to achieve victory. When the need for more comes, if we have the courage … the guts … to do whatever is necessary, we shall not fail. That victory will be the nation's as well as Alaska's … and the world … should deepen our determination to end American colonialism." He also organized a "Committee of One Hundred" prominent Americans who supported statehood. Members of the committee included Pearl S. Buck, James Cagney, Eleanor Roosevelt, and Arthur Schlesinger, Jr.

On April 24, 1956, the people of Alaska went to the polls and resoundingly approved the proposed Constitution by a vote of 17,477 to 8,180. This constitution was rated by the National Municipal League as, "One of the best, if not the best, state constitutions even written." The

National Municipal League (NML) was founded in 1894 by future President Theodore Roosevelt, future Supreme Court Judge Louis Brandeis, and architect Frederick Law Olmsted. The NML was a non-profit group committed to making local governments more open, accessible, and effective. The organization's name was changed to National Civic League in 1986.

With the adoption of the Constitution, Bob Bartlett, William Eaton, and Ernest Gruening increased the pressure on President Eisenhower and Congress to grant statehood. Ted Stevens was now working for the Eisenhower Administration at the Department of the Interior in Washington, D.C. Their case was bolstered by the votes of the people of Alaska. In 1946, residents voted in favor of a referendum for statehood by a margin of 9,630 to 6,822. More than a decade later, statehood was again supported by nearly 84 percent of Alaskans, who on August 26, 1958, voted 40,452 to 8,010.

In 1956, Republicans renominated President Dwight D. Eisenhower for a second term. The Democrats renominated former Illinois Governor Adlai E. Stevenson who had been defeated by the General four years earlier. In addition, the two political parties adopted platforms that are a formal set of policy statements designed to appeal to the general public.

In its platform, Republicans said, "We pledge immediate statehood for

17

Alaska, recognizing the fact that adequate provision for defense requirements must be made." In their version, Democrats said, "These territories (Alaska and Hawaii) have contributed greatly to our national economic and cultural life and are vital to our defense. We of the Democratic Party, therefore, pledge immediate statehood for these two territories."

As a result of the plebiscite, party platforms, and effective lobbying, President Eisenhower finally endorsed Alaska statehood in 1958. According to veteran journalist, Jim Newton who wrote a book in 2011 entitled *Eisenhower: The White House Years*, "Eisenhower had been skeptical of Alaska statehood. The area was so vast, so uninhabited, so removed from the rest of the nation that it hardly seems to warrant consideration. In his view, Hawaii, with its larger population and strategic significance, struck him as a sounder case. There were, moreover, political considerations. It was generally assumed in Washington that Alaska would tilt Democratic and Hawaii would vote Republican." What is ironic is that since statehood, Republicans have controlled the Alaskan delegation, while Hawaii Democrats have held both U.S. Senate and House seats more than 80 percent of the time.

Concurrent with this development, Senate Majority Leader Lyndon B. Johnson assured Bob Bartlett that "Dixiecrats" or Southern Democrats would not filibuster the Alaska bill. The Alaska Territorial legislature also implemented the so-called Tennessee Plan. This plan was first used in May 1798 when the territory of Tennessee voted to send a Congressional delegation to Washington, D.C. without waiting for an enabling act from Congress. This plan was also used to advance statehood in California, Iowa, Kansas, Michigan, and Oregon. The voters of the Alaska territory selected Bob Bartlett and Ernest Gruening to represent them in the U.S. Senate and Ralph J. Rivers to serve in the U.S. House of Representatives. Each of these men presented credentials but were not seated nor allowed to cast a vote.

Despite the endorsement of President Eisenhower, the road to statehood was arduous. In the House of Representatives, the Majority Leader John W. McCormick (D-MA) scheduled the bill over the objections of powerful Rules Committee Chairman, The Honorable Howard W. Smith (D-VA) who strongly opposed Alaskan statehood.

The Majority Leader moved to consider this historic legislation by utilizing House Rule XI, Clause 20. This rule allowed the Chairman of the House Interior and Insular Affairs Committee, Congressman Wayne Aspinall (D-CO), to bring a statehood bill directly to the floor of the House of Representatives as a "privileged measure." It also provided that each of the 435 members of the House could be recognized for up to one hour to argue for or against statehood. Adopted in 1890, Rule XI, Clause 20 was used to bring into the Union Colorado, Nebraska, Nevada, Montana, North Dakota, South Dakota, Washington, and West Virginia.

In his opening remarks on May 21, 1958, the author of H. R. 7999, Congressman Leo O'Brien (D-NY), the Chairman of the House Interior and Insular Affairs Subcommittee on Territorial and Insular Affairs said, "Now I would like to go into the question of what this means to all of us. I think that we could very well today forget this talk of colonialism, forget that Alaska has been hanging fire in the limbo of an unincorporated territory for 90 years, forget the aspirations and hopes of the people there; and think selfishly, if you will, of our own districts and the rest of the nation. I tell you that I believe, as far as my district is concerned, statehood is a must."

In response, Rules Committee Chairman Smith retorted, "This was the greatest giveaway in the history of the country. For the first time in the history of statehood in this nation, we have not reserved to the people of the United States, to whom it belongs, all of the mineral resources in the land that we give to a new state."

After four days of lively debate, Alaska's Delegate Bob Bartlett (D-AK) passionately reminded his colleagues, "Daily I grieve for the citizens there who pay all federal taxes which apply to citizens of the state, who are bound by all federal laws that apply to the citizens of other states but have no right to vote in this Congress of the United States, and who in so many ways occupy inferior status. 90 years ought to be long enough." It had been Bob Bartlett who had asked Congressman Leo O'Brien to move his version of an Alaskan Statehood bill. He felt it was appropriate for a representative of New York with the largest population to assist Alaska that had the smallest population to become our nation's 49th state.

On May 28, 1958, the House of Representatives approved H.R. 7999 by a vote of 210 to 166. Years later, in recognition of his leadership, the State of Alaska named a mountain after Congressman O'Brien's grandson Terrance. In addition, *Life Magazine* opined in an article on Chairman Smith that he was, "A Virginia gentleman whose impeccable manners include little respect for either free enterprise or democracy."

In the U.S. Senate, Majority Leader Lyndon B. Johnson (D-TX) was able to schedule consideration of the House approved H. R. 7999 without it being subjected to a filibuster. The Chairman of the Senate Interior and Insular Affairs Committee, the Honorable James E. Murray (D-MT) gave the first speech on the legislation. Senator Murray said, "The primary reason statehood should be granted Alaska is that the cornerstone of our American tradition is freedom --- freedom to be governed by officials of our own choosing; freedom to participate, on a basis of equality, in the formation of the laws and policies under which we live."

Opponents of the legislation raised three major arguments. The first was articulated by Senator James Eastland (D-AL) who said, "I think the bill violates the constitution of the United States." Senator Willis Robertson (D-VA) argued, "The geographic location of Alaska imposes a permanent handicap to the integration of its population as a homogeneous unit in our Union of States." Finally, Senator Prescott Bush (R-CT), who was the father and grandfather of two Presidents, lamented, "Immediate admission of Alaska into the Union would be harmful --- not helpful, but harmful --- to the people of the territory itself, harmful to the United States, and, therefore, indirectly harmful to the people of my State of Connecticut."

By contrast, Senator Frank Church (D-ID) was a vocal supporter of Alaskan Statehood and he told his colleagues that, "The bill, Mr. President, if passed by the Senate and approved by the President, will constitute the towering achievement of this session, just as the enactment of the civil rights law was the significant accomplishment of the last session." In the last speech prior to voting, Senator Henry "Scoop" Jackson of Washington said on June 30, 1958, "The time is past due for the admission of Alaska to the Union. In any fair appraisal of the Alaska Statehood bill, one fact stands out very clear. This is not a Republican victory; it is not a Democratic victory; it is not simply a victory for Alaska. It is a victory for all Americans and for the democratic process."

When the tally was announced, 64 U.S. Senators had voted for statehood and 20 Senators were opposed. Of that total, 13 "Dixiecrats" including Senators Harry Byrd (D-VA), James Eastland (D-MS), Allen Ellender (D-LA), Sam Ervin (D-NC), William Fullbright (D-AR), John McClellan (D-AR), Richard Russell (D-GA), John Stennis (D-MS), Herman Talmadge (D-GA), and Strom Thurmond (D-SC) voted against the legislation. These were legendary members of the U.S. Senate. It was also interesting that neither Senate Majority Leader Lyndon Johnson nor House Speaker Sam Rayburn, who were both from Texas, voted on the legislation. President Dwight Eisenhower signed the Alaskan Statehood Act into law on July 7, 1958.

Alaska officially became the 49th State on January 3, 1959, when our 34th President issued Proclamation 8269 which stated, "Now, Therefore, I, Dwight D. Eisenhower, President of the United States of America, do hereby declare and proclaim that the procedural requirements imposed by the Congress on the State of Alaska to entitle that state to admission into the Union have been complied with in all respects and that admission of the State of Alaska into the Union on an equal footing with the other states of the Union is now accomplished."

In the 58 years since statehood, a significant number of notable events have occurred in the 49th State. For instance, Alaska has the smallest bicameral state legislature in the nation. On March 27, 1964, Alaska experienced a 9.2 earthquake, the largest in North American history. It caused the deaths of 119 Alaskans and $300 million in damages.

In 1968, the Atlantic Richfield Company announced the discovery of a giant oil field at Prudhoe Bay on the Arctic Coastal Plain. It was one of the greatest oil discoveries in history. Three years later, the Congress passed the Alaska Claims Settlement Act of 1971. One of the features of this Act was the creation of Alaska Native Regional Corporations who are charged with the responsibility of adjudicating claims under the law. Today, there are 13 regional corporations representing Alaskan Tribal interests. This includes Athabaskans, Haidas, Inupiaq Eskimos, Tlingits, and Yupik Eskimos. Some of these claims were directly related to the March 24, 1989 grounding of the 987-foot Exxon Valdez on Bligh Reef, Alaska. As a result of navigational gross negligence, the Exxon Valdez spilled 11 million gallons of oil into the pristine Prince William Sound. This spill was at the time the largest in U.S. history and it cost more than $2 billion to clean up.

Alaska also has the third smallest state population in the United States with 739,818 residents. Only Vermont and Wyoming have fewer folks living within their borders.

In his book *Alaska,* world-renowned author James Michener noted, "Alaska did not produce supermen, but in its formative periods it was served by men of character and determination, and it is fortunate land which knows such public servants." While Alaska may not have superheroes, it has given the nation two legislative giants in the past 40 years, Senator Ted Stevens and Congressman Don Young who is the subject of this book.

By way of full disclosure, I have had the honor of knowing Congressman Don Young since 1981. I have worked for him on two separate occasions. He has literally twice saved me from unemployment and more importantly, his dedication to the people of Alaska is insatiable. No one works harder in the U.S. Congress to improve the lives of their constituents than Don Young. In addition, you always know where Congressman Young stands on a specific policy issue. I have worked for other members of Congress who in their desire not to upset or alienate their constituents would frequently respond to their letters with robotic responses like, "Your input has been noted and will be considered in my decision making process" or worse "Your cogent arguments are appreciated and will be kept in mind." These responses would be sent to the constituent regardless of their position on an issue or specific piece of federal legislation.

During Congressman Young's long and distinguished career, he has taken a key leadership role on some of the most important legislation enacted during the past 50 years. These include: Alaskan Pipeline Act of 1973, Endangered Species Act of 1973, Fishery Conservation and Management Act of 1976, Alaska National Interests Land Conservation Act of 1980, National Wildlife Refuge System Improvement Act of 1997, Migratory Bird Treaty Reform Act of 1998, and the Safe, Accountable, Flexible, Efficient Transportation Equity Act: A Legacy for Users Act of 2005 (SAFETEA-LU).

CHAPTER 1: FORT YUKON'S FAVORITE SON

Donald Edwin "Don" Young was born on June 9, 1933 in Meridian, California. He earned degrees from Yuba and Chico State Colleges. It was at Chico State College where he obtained a bachelor's degree in teaching. From 1955 to 1957, he honorably served this nation as a M-60 tank driver in the 41st tank battalion in Ulm, Germany. This was the eighth year of the Cold War in Europe. It was a terrifying time when school children practiced duck and cover drills, families built bomb shelters in their backyards, and most Americans lived in fear of a nuclear attack.

The 41st tank battalion, affectionately known as the Thunderbirds, was activated on August 15, 1942 at Camp Polk, Louisiana. Members of this elite battalion served with General George S. Patton, Jr, whose Third Army successful saved thousands of U.S. troops during the famous Battle of the Bulge.

It takes an extraordinary person to live in Alaska. The moniker "The Last Frontier" is more than just a motto. Alaska has an extremely harsh environment with brutal weather and for many residents a lack of sufficient doctors, law enforcement, teachers, and indoor plumbing. Those who move to the 49th state deeply value personal liberty, privacy, and limited government.

They love this country but want to be left alone to enjoy Alaska's stunning beauty, its vast wilderness, and abundant wildlife. It is the only state I have visited where you can see parked in residential driveways, boats, cars, trucks, and personal aircraft.

Don Young is one of those extraordinary Americans who embraced the Alaskan lifestyle. After completing his military service, he drove his brand new 1959 pink Plymouth Fury 3,602 miles from Meridian, California to Fairbanks, Alaska. After an arduous ten-day drive, he arrived in the state's second most populated city. There were no jobs available. He then drove his beloved Fury the 350 miles to Anchorage.

After working as a firefighter, structural engineer, and homebuilder, Don Young was offered a teaching position in Fort Yukon, Alaska. This remote village is seven miles above the Arctic Circle and today it has a population of about 700 people. The Principal of the Old BIA State School, Dr. Gray, offered him the job. While he was trained to be a coach at the high school level, Dr. Gray advised him that the school did not have a gymnasium. Despite this fact, Don Young became the first coach ever hired above the Arctic Circle.

What the school did have were native Alaskan children who were eager to obtain an education. On that first day, he walked into the classroom and found 25 5th grade students who were sitting at attention. The room had a wood stove to keep them from freezing, and old fashion desks with inkwells and quill pens. For the next eight years, he taught his students Geography, History, Mathematics, and Science. As he said to me, we learned together and these students had an insatiable appetite for knowledge. Four of his students attended college.

Don Young was also a riverboat captain, a licensed mariner and a barge owner. As a barge operator, he delivered vital supplies to the residents of Beaver, Fort Yukon, Galena, Grayling, and Koyukuk. He even made a trip to Nome, Alaska, which is 592 miles west of Fort Yukon, Alaska. While his life was challenging, nothing seemed to slow him down. At one point, he was working as a barge owner, teacher, trapper, and a member of the Alaska Legislature.

He met and married a bookkeeper named Lu Fredson who was the daughter of one of the state's most prominent Alaskan natives. John Fredson was the first Athabascan man to graduate from college and one of the first to successfully climb Denali Mountain. Lu Young was a force of nature. During their 48 years of marriage, she was Don Young's greatest supporter, strategist, and defender. While sadly this remarkable woman passed away in 2009, those who had the privilege of meeting her will always remember her fondly.

In the fall of 1964, Don Young filed as one of the three candidates for the office of Mayor of Fort Yukon. This was a two-year elected position. Upon his election, he dedicated himself to getting things done for his constituents. In politics, there are two types of representatives. The first are "Show Horses" who love to see their picture and words in the news. The second are "Work Horses" who are not interested in media attention but in improving the lives they were elected to represent. To this day, Don Young remains a "Work Horse." With a budget of only $5,000, Mayor Young worked tirelessly to ensure the residents of Fort Yukon had access to improved law enforcement and other essential public services.

On November 8, 1966, Mayor Don Young was one of 14 candidates running for District 16 in the Alaska House of Representatives. He was elected to the House with 5,287 votes. This multi-member district contained 14 precincts in Fairbanks whose citizens' cast more than 40 percent of the total number of votes.

Prior to taking office, however, a number of newly elected House members including Nicholas Begich, George H. Hohman, and Don Young were advised that Article II, Section 5 of the Constitution of the State of Alaska prohibited dual office holding by legislators. Specifically, its says, "No legislator may hold any other office or position of profit under the United States or the State."

These men worked for the Alaska public school system. Because of their love of teaching, they decided to petition for relief from the Alaska Supreme Court. Don Young was represented by future Alaska U.S. Senator Ted Stevens. On May 17, 1968, the Alaska Supreme Court ruled against appellants Nicholas Begich, George H. Hohman, and Donald E. Young in the Begich v Jefferson case. Writing for the court, Supreme Court Justice Jay Rabinowitz opined, "Alaska's constitutional prohibition against members of our three separate branches of state government holding any other positions of profit under the State of Alaska reflects the intent to guard against conflict of interest, self-aggrandizement, concentration of power, and dilution of separation of powers."

While teachers are state employees, it is ridiculous to suggest that the appellants in this case were interested in self-aggrandizement or concentration of power. What they were interested in was educating the children of Alaska. These men did not become teachers to become rich, powerful, or create any conflict of interest. They were dedicated public servants who cared deeply about their students.

On November 5, 1968, Don Young was re-elected to further represent the citizens of District 16. This time, he finished first among 14 candidates with

7,349 out of 12,561 votes cast, nearly 60 percent of the total.

During the four years in the Alaska House of Representatives, Don Young served as the Chairman of the Commerce Committee. He introduced and co-sponsored 84 pieces of legislation. Of that total, Governors of Alaska signed 14 into law. Among his approved measures were bills providing state aid for agricultural fairs, construction of rural and state libraries, creation of a public defender agency, incentives for the discovery and production of certain minerals, the regulation and certification of air carriers, and a small grain incentive program.

During his service, he was part of a coalition with Representatives Gene Guess and Joe McGill who wanted to improve the lives of all Alaskans. Their motto was: "Let's make a Deal." As a result of this relationship, he has fondly described his four-year tenure in the Alaska House of Representatives.

On November 3, 1970, Representative Don Young was elected to the Alaska State Senate for District 1. In this election, he received 7,051 votes out of 12,934 casts. When all ballots were counted there were 10 Republican and 10 Democrat members of the Alaska Senate.

According to Don Young, the Democrats selected Howard C. Bradshaw to serve as Senate President and the

Republicans choose Jay Hammond. After remaining deadlocked for four days, the Democrats suggested a secret ballot. When these votes were counted, State Senator Hammond prevailed on an 11 to 9 vote. He became the Senate President for the 7th Alaska Legislature.

During his two years in the Senate, Don Young served on the Senate Commerce and Resources Committees. He introduced and co-sponsored 48 bills. Of these measures, Governor William Allen Egan signed 13 into law. Among his efforts were the creation of notary public seals, dental insurance coverage, state matching funds for sports facilities, teachers' compensation, and uniform standards for alcoholism and intoxication treatment. Unlike his fond memories of his House service, Senator Don Young found the State Senate to be a frustrating institution. This was because of the Senate's inability to get enough things done for the citizens of Alaska.

During his service in the Alaska legislature, elected members were not assigned dedicated staff. The Legislative Services Office was responsible for preparing all legislative text. Elected members had to develop their own legislative ideas; write their own letters, statements, and press releases; and negotiate directly with their colleagues to move their bills forward. This placed a premium on interpersonal relationships.

As the election of 1972 approached, a number of prominent Alaskan Republicans calculated their chances of defeating freshman Congressman Nick Begich. He had won the seat two years earlier when he soundly defeated future U.S. Senator and future Alaskan Governor Frank Murkowski by more than 8,000 votes. After careful analysis, they decided not to run against him.

State Senator Don Young, with the enthusiastic support of his wife Lu, carefully contemplated whether to challenge his friend Nick Begich who was widely popular throughout the state. After announcing his candidacy, he ran a spirited and hard fought campaign.

Sadly, less than a month before the election, a plane carrying Congressman Begich, House Majority Leader Hale Boggs, staffer Russell Brown, and pilot Don Jonz was lost in the Alaskan wilderness. What is known is that on October 16, 1972, a Cessna 310 with the registration number N1812H left Anchorage for a flight to Juneau, Alaska. The purpose of the trip was to attend a fundraiser for Congressman Begich. His special guest for the event was the powerful Majority Leader Hale Boggs (D-LA). The weather for the flight in mid-October was fog, drizzle, and low clouds.

After failing to arrive in Juneau, the Air Force, Coast Guard, and Navy conduced a massive search for the plane. It was at the time the largest in U.S. history. The search lasted 39 days, it covered 325,000 square miles, and there was never any sighting of the plane or its occupants.

What was interesting in this case was the pilot, Don Jonz, who was an experienced aviator. Several days after the plane's disappearance, the U.S. Coast Guard issued a communications stating, "Regarding the pilot: the pilot is very independent. He is known by local pilots to apparently not "Fly by the Book."

This assessment was confirmed by Don Jonz himself who penned an article that was ironically published in the October 1972 edition of *Flying Magazine*." In an article entitled, "*Ice Without Fear*," Don Jonz wrote, "Playing with ice is like playing with the devil, fun, but don't play unless you can cheat. If you are sneaky, smart, and careful, you can fly 350 days a year and disregard 99 percent of the bullshit you hear about icing."

On November 7, 1972, Alaskan citizens went to the polls and re-elected Nick Begich by nearly 12,000 votes. While the Congressman was supported throughout the state, Senator Don Young did comfortably win in a number of rural communities including Adak, Butte, Chugiak, For Wainwright, Matanuska, Palmer, Richardson, Wasilla, and his hometown of Fort Yukon. Although there is no way to determine how the disappearance of Congressman Begich's plane on October 16, 1972, affected the final outcome on Election Day.

On December 29, 1972, the four passengers on the Cessna 310 were declared dead. As a result of this tragedy, Congress mandated the installation of emergency locator transmitters for all U.S. civil aircraft. Governor Egan scheduled a Special Election to fill the vacant Congressional seat on March 6, 1973. The two candidates were State Senator Don Young and the President of the Alaska Federation of Natives, Emil Notti. On Election Day, 68,167 Alaskans went to the polls. There were 35,044 votes cast for Senator Young and 33,123 votes for Emil Notti. This was a margin of less than 2,000 votes.

Eight days later, Don Young was sworn-in as a member of the 93rd Congress. With the adoption of H. Res. 305, introduced by Republican Leader Gerald R. Ford (R-MI), Congressman Young was assigned to the following Committees: Interior and Insular Affairs and Merchant Marine and Fisheries. He was appointed to the House Public Works and Transportation Committee in 1995.

The real work of all legislature bodies occurs within its standing Committees. It is here where ideas are analyzed and examined in public hearings and voting sessions known as mark-ups. Under normal procedures, only if a majority of the relevant Committee supports the idea will it be considered by the entire legislative body. This is how our "Laws Are Made."

On his swear-in day, Congressman Bill Young (R-FL), who represented Florida's 13th District for 42 years, greeted the new member Don Young. In his statement, Bill Young said, "As one Young to another, I can assure him that his presence will be well noted and long remembered --- particularly by confused telephone operators, mailmen, and sundry others trying to figure one Congressman Young from another." There were six Congressmen Young in the 93rd Congress. It didn't take long, however, for people to sit up and take notice of the gentleman from Alaska.

As proof of that assessment, Congressman Young introduced 33 bills during the 93rd Congress. His first bill was introduced on April 3, 1973. This measure, H.R. 6540, authorized an appropriation of $150,000 to assist the Arctic Winter Games in the State of Alaska. In his maiden speech, Congressman Young noted, "For as these games progress and grow, they will expand to provide a forum for international peace and understanding between the young people of all northern nations and territories."

In 1969, there was an agreement signed by Alaska Governor Walter Hickel, Canadian Commissioner Stuart Hodgson, and Canadian Commissioner James Smith to initiate the games. The first games were held in Yellowknife in the Northwest Territories in 1970. The idea was to provide an opportunity for athletes from the circumpolar north to compete on their own terms.

While this bill was not enacted into law, four other Don Young measures were approved. These included legislation for: the relief of Michael A. Korhonen, to document the vessel *Miss Keku* to engage in American fisheries, to amend the Merchant Marine Act of 1936 to define the term "noncontiguous trade" to include trade between Alaska, Hawaii, Puerto Rico, and the other territories, and to allow the sale of certain federal property to the Gospel Missionary Union in Alaska.

The private relief bill, H.R. 7089, waived the statue of limitations to allow Michael Korhonen of Juneau, Alaska to obtain compensation from the U.S. Coast Guard. Korhonen was an authorized observer on a Coast Guard plane. This aircraft crashed on June 15, 1967 during a search and rescue mission and he suffered injuries and damages.

As someone who spent nearly 40 years working in the House of Representatives, I can categorically state that it is a rare occurrence for a freshman member to have even one public law enacted. In the 93rd Congress, Don Young had four federal statutes. It is, therefore, not surprising that his Republican colleagues honored him as the "Freshman Congressman of the Year."

In addition to those four public laws, Don Young introduced important legislation dealing with fishing in U.S. waters, marine fisheries, Outer Continental Shelf revenues, ship mortgages, and U.S. oil imports. On April 9, 1973, he proposed H.R. 6756, the Trans-Alaskan Pipeline Authorization Act.

For the next seven months, Congressman Young worked tirelessly to convince Members of Congress that it was essential to build an environmentally safe means to transport the anticipated billions of barrels of Prudhoe Bay oil to Valdez, Alaska. He was rewarded for his efforts when the House leadership decided to consider H.R. 9130, introduced by Congressman John Melcher (D-MT) who was the Chairman of the Public Lands Subcommittee. This was one of 30 measures dealing with the pipeline issue.

Under the Melcher Trans-Alaskan Pipeline Act proposal, the Secretary of Interior was authorized to grant a right-of-way to the pipeline and to issue necessary permits for its construction, operation, and maintenance; Congress was required to approve the export of any North Slope oil; pipeline materials must be manufactured in the United States; and pipeline owners must pay all pollution costs and any damages to aquatic life, private or public property, and wildlife.

This legislation was critical because approval of the pipeline had been prevented by administrative delays, judicial injunctions, and the decision of the United States Court of Appeals for the District of Columbia in the Wilderness Society v Morton case. In its February 9, 1973 opinion the court blocked the issuance of government permits. The essence of the Court's objection was that the permit issued by Secretary Rogers Morton exceeded the width of the right-of-way allowed under the Mineral Leasing Act of 1920.

Writing for the court, Judge J. Skelly Wright opined, "We have no more power to grant this request than we have, the power to increase Congressional appropriations. The power over the public laws thus entrusted to Congress is without limitation." Two months later, the U.S. Supreme Court declined to review the decision.

However, before the House could act on the legislation, the U.S. Senate began its own consideration of a similar bill, S. 1081, introduced by Senator Henry "Scoop" Jackson. In his opening remarks, Senator Jackson warned his colleagues that, "The critical energy shortage points up the critical need to begin construction of the pipeline as soon as possible so that the vast oil resources of the North Slope of Alaska will be available to help meet our urgent energy needs and reduce our growing dependence on uncertain, insecure, and politically motivated foreign sources of crude oil."

While American motorists had long enjoyed the availability of cheap gasoline, the United States was growing increasingly dependent on Middle East oil. Long gas lines at your local filing stations had become a reality. To many Americans, these lines were an annoying inconvenience.

Within the next year, however, this annoyance became much more sinister. In 1973, in response to the U.S. position on the Yom Kippur War, 12 Arab oil-producing countries declared an oil embargo on this nation. In response, the Congress established oil price controls and American motorists got to enjoy odd-even rationing of gas based on a car's license plate. It was vital that this nation embrace energy independence and the pipeline was an indispensable component of that plan.

A second speaker in support of S. 1081 was the Senior Senator from Alaska Ted Stevens. In his statement, he noted that, "The need for the pipeline has been known for years, and I have continued to warn my colleagues of the absolute necessity of the trans-Alaskan pipeline as the energy crisis has grown more and more severe – not only here in the United States but throughout the world."

During the two weeks of Senate debate, there were a number of amendments offered to S. 1081. Without question, the most important was the one offered by Senators Mike Gravel and Ted Stevens of Alaska. This amendment stipulated that Congress grant a right-of-way for the pipeline, airport, and road; it directed the Secretary of Interior to issue all necessary permits; and it declared that the granting of these rights was not reviewable by the courts.

Without this language, it is likely the pipeline construction would have been further delayed by endless legal challenges from the environmental community. They were not going to give up the fight and this is reflected by their all out effort to defeat the Gravel-Stevens Amendment. In fact, they almost succeeded. When the final tally was announced the amendment was adopted by a 49 to 48 vote. However, Senator Allen Cranston (D-CA) had missed the vote and was strongly opposed to the amendment.

Under legislative procedures, there is always a motion to recommit. In this case, there was a motion to table and retain the Gravel-Stevens Amendment. This motion was agreed to by a vote of 50 to 49 when Vice President Spiro Agnew voted for the motion to table. On final passage, S. 1081 was approved by the U.S. Senate on a 77 to 20 vote.

This was the second and last time Vice President Agnew broke a tie vote in the Senate. The first such vote occurred on August 6, 1969 on an amendment affecting the Anti Ballistic Missile System offered by Senator Margaret Chase Smith (R-ME).

Under our constitution, Article 1, Sec. 3 stipulates, "The Vice President of the United States shall be President of the Senate, but shall have no vote, unless they be equally divided." To date, there have been 264 tie-breaking votes since 1789. Vice President John Adams leads the list with 29 tie breaking votes. There are 12 Vice Presidents, including Joe Biden, who had no tie breaking votes.

On July 28, 1973, the House Committee on Interior and Insular Affairs favorably reported H.R. 9130 to the House of Representatives by voice vote. Five days later, the bill was debated in the People's House. In his opening remarks, Chairman Melcher told his colleagues, "The first point is that the need for both Title I and Title II of this bill is urgent. The worsening energy crisis, our economic well-being, and our national security are all involved."

In his opening statement on the legislation, Congressman Don Young said, "Today we have the opportunity to make another great decision affecting Alaska, a decision that will have ramifications for the entire nation, a decision that will effectively demonstrate Congress' determination to bring about a solution to the energy problems with which we are now confronted."

House Republican Leader Gerald R. Ford (R-MI) concluded his floor statement by saying, "Let us move ahead with the Trans-Alaskan Pipeline. No longer should the will of the American people be frustrated. We need the Alaska pipeline, and we need it now."

By contrast, Congressman John Dingell (D-MI) argued, "The bill is far too broad in its sweeping authority and it is not limited to the Alaskan pipeline, but it also applies to the public lands and forest and wildlife reserved on the lower 48 states."

During consideration in the House, a number of amendments were debated. Perhaps the most interesting was one offered by the gentleman from Michigan John Dingell. His amendment simply stated that the pipeline bill and its provisions would only apply to Alaska. The amendment was defeated by a vote of 160 to 261. H.R. 9130 was ultimately approved by an overwhelming vote of 358 to 60.

In Mid-November 1973, both the House and the Senate agreed to the Conference Report on S. 1081. A Conference Report is a document prepared to reflect how a piece of legislation has been modified when members of the two bodies met to resolve the various differences in the bill. In this case, the House adopted the Report 301 to 14 and the Senate followed suit with an 80 to 5 vote. This historic measure would not have been adopted without the tireless efforts of the Alaska delegation.

On November 16, 1973, President Richard M. Nixon signed the Trans-Alaskan Pipeline Act into law. It became Public Law 93-153. According to Congressman Don Young, "Next to statehood itself, the most historical legislation passed that affected every Alaskan then, now, and in the future, was the passage of the pipeline legislation."

Four months later, freshman Congressman Young addressed a Joint Session of the Alaska State Legislature. In his remarks, he noted that, "Congress cleared the way for the pipeline after a long, hard fight. I'm proud to have played a role in winning that fight, but I couldn't have done it without the solid backing and help Alaskans gave me, the Governor and members of the legislature who came to Washington to help me present Alaska's case, the Alaskans who talked about Alaska and the pipeline during their travels across the country and the Alaskans who wrote letters to friends. When I came to Congress, the odds were decidedly against the pipeline."

Once the pipeline right-of-way and the more than 1,300 necessary permits were obtained, Alyeska began construction on April 29, 1974. The first pipe was laid at the Tonsina River on March 27, 1975. The final pipe was welded on March 27, 1975. Oil began flowing on June 20, 1977 and on August 1*; the *ARCO Juneau* was the first tanker to carry North Slope crude oil.

In terms of the overall impact, the 800-mile pipeline crossed 34 major rivers, 800 smaller streams, and the Alaska, Brooks, and Chugach Mountain Ranges. The construction of the pipeline required some 70,000 workers and it cost $8 billion to build. The Alyeska Pipeline Service Company privately funded the vast majority of this money. The Atlantic Richfield Company, British Petroleum, and Humble Oil Company established this consortium in 1970. Sadly, 32 workers were killed during pipeline construction.

As of January 1, 2017, the Trans-Alaskan Pipeline System (TAPS) has transported about 18 billion barrels of oil, 12,000 tankers have been escorted through Prince William Sound, and more than $54 billion has been deposited in the Alaska Permanent Fund. This fund was created in 1976 as Article IX, Section 15 of the Alaska Constitution. It was established to ensure that each Alaskan received long-term benefits that oil development would bring to the state. The first fund deposit was $734,000 in February 1977.

According to scientists at the University of Michigan, "The Trans-Alaskan Pipeline is well worth the environmental risks because of the minimal damage it does, and it is the most realistic, convenient, and sustainable way to transport out of Northern Alaska." Between 1977 and 2015, about 291,000 out of 18 billion barrels of oil were spilled. The pipeline has had an outstanding environmental record and neither the 170 bird species nor the Central Arctic Caribou Herd have been adversely affected."

While Congress is frequently criticized for their actions or inactions, the authorization of the Trans-Alaskan Pipeline was one of the institution's finest moments.

CHAPTER 2: EVOLUTION OF ENDANGERED SPECIES ACT

With the end of World War II, the American people became increasingly concerned about the quality of the air they breathed, the water they drank, and the disappearance of popular wildlife. On September 27, 1962, an obscure marine biologist who worked for the U.S. Fish and Wildlife Service published *Silent Spring.*

As a member of the Alaska Legislature, Don Young, who has been a lifelong conservationist, worked to ensure his constituents had a bright future that included clean air, healthy drinking water, and sustainable wildlife populations.

The fundamental premise of Rachel Carson's novel was that certain pesticides were causing harmful effects on the environment. Specifically, pesticides, like DDT, were killing avian species including our national symbol, the bald eagle. While DDT was very effective in controlling mosquitoes, its residue washed into our waterways. Aquatic plants and fish absorbed it. Unfortunately, Bald eagles, Brown pelicans, Osprey, and Peregrine Falcons ate these fish and were poisoned by the pesticide. DDT also interfered with the bird's ability to produce strong eggshells. This thinning caused them to either break or fail to hatch.

The banning of DDT by the Environmental Protection Agency in 1972 was highly beneficial to avian wildlife. Sadly, this action caused a terrible unintended consequence. For years, DDT has been a cost effective method to kill malaria-carrying mosquitoes throughout the undeveloped world.

This presented a societal dilemma. By banning the use of DDT, millions of birds and their offspring were saved. But this decision didn't happen in a vacuum. Those working within the Environmental Protection Agency knew that by prohibiting this pesticide people would die. And, in fact, they have. Millions in Nigeria, the Democratic Republic of the Congo, Mozambique, Burkina Faso, and Sierra Leone have lost their lives because of malaria. The vast majority of victims have been children and pregnant women.

It is undeniable that Rachel Carson's best selling book was a watershed event in this country. It stimulated the birth of the environmental movement, produced additional federal protections for the Bald eagle, resulted in the creation of the Environmental Protection Agency in 1970, and the designation of April 23, 1970 as "Earth Day." Since its publication, tens of millions of copies in almost 20 different languages have been sold. It is required reading for all employees of the U.S. Fish and Wildlife Service and biology students throughout the world.

The American people have always had tremendous affection for wildlife, which holds a special place in our hearts. This is why millions of our citizens photograph wildlife, visit zoos and parks like Animal Kingdom, Busch Gardens, and Sea World, and watch nature films. Huge sums of money are spent on safaris to observe and photograph wild elephants, hippos, lions, and rhinos in Kenya, South Africa, and Zimbabwe. They also agree with my friend Dr. Jane Goodall that, "If we kill off the wild, then we are killing a part of our souls."

In the mid-1960's, Americans were shocked to learn that some of this nation's iconic species were headed towards extinction. They found it incomprehensible that within the continental United States, there were only 27 California condors, 54 Whooping cranes, 271 Grizzly bears, 324 Peregrine falcons, and 416 Bald eagles.

As a result of this rapidly disappearing wildlife, the U.S. Congress responded. On June 23, 1966, the House of Representatives considered the Endangered Species Preservation Act. This Act was sponsored by Congressman T. Ashton Thompson (D-LA) who was the Chairman of the Merchant Marine Subcommittee on Fisheries and Wildlife Conservation. The goal of this measure was to, "Conserve, protect, restore, and propagate certain species of native fish and wildlife." This was to be accomplished by requiring the Secretary of the Interior to produce a list of endangered vertebrates within the United States. These species would be protected whenever possible and convenient.

After passing both the House and the Senate, the Conference Report was considered on October 13, 1966 in the People's House. Congressman John Dingell, who was the floor manager of the legislation noted, "I will state the bill comes unanimously from the Committee. The Senate overwhelmingly passed it. The statement of managers on the House was unanimously agreed to, and is signed by every single conferee on both sides of the aisle." After both legislative bodies completed action on the bill, President Lyndon B. Johnson signed it into law on March 9, 1966. Public Law 89-669 was the predecessor to the Endangered Species Act.

As required, the Secretary of Interior published a list of the first species designated as endangered in the *Federal Register*. There were 36 birds, 22 fishes, 14 mammals, and 6 reptiles and amphibians on the "Class of 1967" list. Among the listed species were the alligator, Bald eagle, California candor, Grizzly bear, and Whooping crane.

Just three years later, the Congress considered the Endangered Species Act of 1969. This was far more restrictive than the previous law. It prohibited the importation of any species determined to be threatened with extinction on a worldwide basis; it made it unlawful to knowingly put into interstate or foreign commerce any species taken contrary to federal, state, or foreign laws; it authorized up to $15 million to the Secretary of the Interior to acquire privately owned lands for the conservation and protection of species; and it allocated up to $200,000 for an International Wildlife Conference.

Like the 1966 law, both the House of Representatives and the U.S. Senate, with little debate and no opposition, overwhelmingly adopted this bill. One of the few members who did speak on H.R. 11363 was the Republican floor manager, Congressman Thomas Pelly (R-WA). In his remarks, Thomas Pelly said, "The Endangered Species law has been a valuable tool enabling the Secretary of the Interior to identify and take steps to preserve a large number of mammals, birds, and fish which would otherwise soon disappear from the U.S. The scope of the Endangered Species law is, however, unwisely restrictive, and its enforcement and penalty provisions are inadequate." President Richard M. Nixon signed the bill into law on October 20, 1969 (P.L. 91-135).

At the beginning of the 93rd Congress, federal lawmakers were again ready to address the issue of endangered species. Under the terms of the Endangered Species Act of 1973, the U.S. Fish and Wildlife Service was authorized to determine whether certain species warranted listing as threatened or endangered; the possession, taking, transport, and sale of endangered species was prohibited; cooperative agreements and grants to the states who establish threatened and endangered species programs was authorized; and rewards would be paid to those providing information on violations of the Act. It also provided statutory listing authority to the Department of Commerce and required a study on endangered plants.

During consideration in the House, the bill sponsor, John Dingell stated, "H.R. 37 amends and extends laws now on the books: endangered species legislation enacted in 1966 and 1969. The existing laws are sound, as far as they go, but later events have shown that they do not go far enough. Present law needs to be more flexible, to adapt themselves to the animals themselves and to deal with problems which did not exist until a few years ago." This is a classic example of how our legislative branch operates. You start with a simple solution to solve a real problem. The law is then revised to make it broader and more comprehensive.

Despite growing restrictions, Don Young supported the legislation because the emphasis remained on saving iconic species without adversely affecting private property owners. There was no mandatory requirement to designate critical habitat for a listed species. As a new member of the House Merchant Marine and Fisheries

Committee, he was actively involved in the drafting of this legislation. He also agreed with his senior Alaskan Senator Ted Stevens "While this bill is not perfect, it takes a major step in the protection of American endangered and threatened species." As a true conservationist, Don Young felt these incremental changes were necessary.

H.R. 37 was signed into law on December 28, 1973. It became Public Law 93-205. It was not a coincidence that President Richard M. Nixon also signed the Clean Water Act of 1972, the Ocean Dumping Act of 1972, and the Clean Air Act of 1973. Along with the Endangered Species Act, these were comprehensive, popular, and powerful environmental statutes.

On March 3, 1973, 80 countries met in Washington, D.C. to negotiate the details of the Convention on International Trade in Endangered Species of Wild Fauna and Flora (CITES). Part of the funding for the conference was allocated by the United States as directed by the Endangered Species Act of 1969.

CITES entered into force in July 1975. There are now 5,000 species of animals and 29,000 species of plants that are protected from over-exploitation. There are 183 countries who are members of CITES and any one of them can propose either increased or decreased protections for a single species or a group of species.

CITES is the only global treaty whose sole focus is the protection of plant and animal species. There are three levels of protection. Appendix I is the most restrictive. It bans all commercial international trade on species afforded this protection. There are approximately 1,200 species on this list including Asian elephants, cheetahs, chimpanzees, manatees, tigers, and Western gorillas.

Appendix II is for species not currently threatened with extinction but they may become endangered if trade is not regulated. In order to transport an Appendix II species, a shipper must obtained necessary export or import permits. There are 21,000 species protected in this category including the American black bear, Emperor scorpion, Great White shark, and Hartmann's Mountain Zebra.

Finally, Appendix III species are those for which a CITES member has regulations within their country "for the purposes of preventing or restricting exploitation, and as needing the cooperation of other parties in control of trade." There are some 170 species on this list including African civets, Alligator snapping turtles, and the two-toed sloth. In its 42 years, CITES has worked diligently and effectively to save a variety of foreign species found throughout the world. This emphasis has eliminated the need for the United States to domestically list foreign species.

By 1988, there was still widespread support for the Endangered Species Act. However, a growing number of House members felt activist federal judges and federal regulations that ignored the letter and spirit of the Act were perverting the law. While the mandatory establishment of critical habitat had become a feature of the law in 1978, massive amounts of private land had not been designated. In fact, the Reagan Administration issued a regulation that limited the protective status of critical habitat. Federal courts ultimately struck down this regulation in the late 1990's.

During the debate on the 1988 Amendments, Don Young told his colleagues, "As one of the originators of the Endangered Species Act, let me say that when we first structured this Act, we had thought that this would be an act to protect and perpetuate species." He went on to say, "After due studies, consultations, and very frankly, with consideration of human beings, from the time of the passage of the Act it has been misused, abused, and used as a tactic by those who oppose many worthwhile human projects to delay those projects."

It was his hope that H. R. 1467, the Endangered Species Act Amendments of 1988 would help to restore the law's original goals. Under this legislation, introduced by the Subcommittee Chairman Gerry Studds (D-MA), the U.S. Fish and Wildlife Service was directed to identify candidate species for listing;

allowed the continued sale of existing inventories of scrimshaw from Alaska; provide additional protections for endangered or threatened plants; increase the penalties for violating the law; delay for two years the mandatory use of turtle excluder devices in the inshore waters of the Atlantic Ocean and the Gulf of Mexico; and authorized up to $85 million for listing, consultations, and recovery of species under the Act.

The bill was fiercely debate on the floor of the House of Representatives. Several important amendments were offered. These included one presented by Congressman Wes Watkins (D-OK) who wanted to remove the leopard darter fish from the Endangered Species Act. This species had caused harm to some of his constituents in Oklahoma. This was clearly an uphill battle since it only affected a handful of Congressional districts and no species had been added or removed from listing by the Congress.

A second amendment was an effort by Congressman Solomon Ortiz (D-TX) to extend throughout the Atlantic Ocean and the Gulf of Mexico the two-year delay on the mandatory use of turtle excluder devices. There were hundreds of shrimpers in Louisiana and Texas who strongly felt these devices resulted in significant catch losses because both shrimp and turtles escaped through the nets opening. This opening was created so that turtles, which frequently drown in the process of fishing for shrimp, had an opportunity to swim safety out of the trawl net.

Congressman Ron Packard (R-CA), who wanted to give discretion to the Secretary of the Interior to consider the protection of human lives, offered the third amendment. Throughout the Act's existence, Congress has always given priority to plants and animals and not human beings. During debate on the Packard Amendment Don Young noted, "Now I heard on the floor today numerous people say that there cannot be any amendments to the Endangered Species Act. Now, whoever said this was a perfect Act? Has it worked? Yes, in many cases, it has but I submit to you through regulations it has been misused and abused. All the gentleman is asking is for the Secretary to have the right to consider the human factor. What is wrong with that?"

Sadly, the majority of the historic 100th Congress was not persuaded and each of the three amendments was handily defeated. Despite being a co-sponsor of H.R. 1467, Don Young voted in favor of these efforts to improve the law. Upon completion of the amendment process, the House on a 399 to 16 vote approved the measure. Seven months later, the U.S. Senate voted 93 to 2 to adopt the bill with a few changes.

After resolving its differences in a House and Senate Conference Committee, the House of Representatives gave its final approval of H.R. 1467 on October 26, 1988. At that time, Don Young stated that, "I rise in support of the Conference Report. This report before us fairly resolves those differences and includes within the agreement of both bodies the text of the African Elephant Conservation Act. Congressmen Don Young and Jack Fields (R-TX) had convinced their colleagues to incorporate this landmark conservation proposal.

The purpose of the African Elephant Conservation Act was to authorize the collection of data from all ivory producing countries to determine the level and their compliancy in poaching; direct the Secretary of Interior to establish a moratorium on raw and worked ivory; and it established an African Elephant Conservation Fund. President George H. Bush used this law in 1989 to stop the importation of all worked elephant ivory products into the United States.

The U.S. is also the only one that provides a small amount of taxpayer money through the African Elephant Conservation Fund to assist range countries in their efforts to save this keystone species. To date, the U.S. Fish and Wildlife Service has approved 450 grants to nations throughout Africa. This money is being effectively spent to stop the elephant's slide toward extinction.

The Conference Report also included Section 2202 (e) which states, "The Secretary shall not established any moratorium under this Section, pursuant to a petition or otherwise, which prohibits the importation into the United States of sport-hunted trophies from elephants that are legally taken by the importer or the importer's principal in an ivory producing country that has submitted an ivory quota." This provision was strongly supported by the hunting and conservation communities. Don Young championed this legislation because he understood that wildlife must have an economic value. Without any value, there is no incentive for indigenous populations to conserve them into their natural habitat.

To most Americans, elephants are beautiful and majestic creatures. To those living with them in Africa, they are a marauding pest that drinks their water, terrorizes their children, and tramples their crops. Unless there is some financial incentive to protect them, these villagers are more than likely to kill rather than save an elephant.

The Conference Report was approved by voice vote. President Ronald W. Reagan signed H.R. 1467 into law on October 7, 1988. It is Public Law 100-478.

The Congress has not passed any comprehensive Endangered Species Act legislation in almost 30 years. In 2004, however, the U.S. military was facing a serious training crisis. As the result of the designation of thousands of acres of military land as critical habitat, it was becoming virtually impossible to properly train Army and Marine Corps recruits.

The poster child for this crisis was Marine Corps Base Camp Pendleton in San Diego, County, California. Since 1942, this camp has trained millions of members of our military forces. Pendleton was built on a wide swath of coastal land and extensive salt marsh habitat. It is breeding grounds for the California Gnatcatcher and Western Snowy Plover. It is also home for the listed Pacific Pocket mouse and Stephens' Kangaroo rat. By 2004, only 500 yards out of 40 miles of beach were open for training. The U.S. Fish and Wildlife Service had classified the rest as "critical habitat" for these four listed species. I remember thinking this was ridiculous. We were sending our troops in harm's way in the Middle East without receiving the life saving training they needed in order to protect two birds and two rodent species.

In an effort to assist the military, then House Natural Resources Committee Chairman Richard Pombo (R-CA) introduced H.R. 1497. Specifically, this bill amended Section 101 of the Sikes Act of 1960. It stipulated, "This Section would prohibit further designations of critical habitat for endangered species in areas for which an integrate natural resource management plan (INRMPS) has been prepared." These plans must be formally reviewed every five years and they are mutually negotiated by the U.S. Fish and Wildlife Service, the National Marine Fisheries Service, and the appropriate state fish and game agency.

The fundamental goals of INRMPS are to assist installation commanders in their efforts to conserve and rehabilitate natural resources and to balance the use of air, land, and water resources for military training and testing with the need to conserve wildlife resources for future generations. The expectation was that military bases, like Pendleton, would be given increased acreage for training by substituting an approved Integrate Natural Resource Management Plan for critical habitat designations. The Department of Defense has jurisdiction over more than 400 military installations. These bases provide habitat for nearly 300 federally listed and threatened species.

After favorably reporting H.R. 1497 from the Natural Resources Committee, it was incorporated within the National Defense Authorization Act for fiscal year 2004. On May 22, 2003, Congressman Wayne T. Gilchrest (R-MD) who was the Chairman of the Subcommittee on Fisheries Conservation, Wildlife, and Oceans told his House colleagues, "So we have improved ESA. We have improved the Marine Mammal Protection Act. We have improved the Sikes Act which protects conservation on 25 million acres of land, and we have improved America's ability to train young people that go into harm's way."

Wayne Gilchrest who represented Maryland's Eastern Shore is a highly decorated marine and he was a leading environmentalist in the Congress. He once roundly criticized Frank Perdue, who was a major employer in his district, for polluting the Chesapeake Bay.

President George W. Bush signed the National Defense Authorization Act into law on November 24, 2003. It became Public Law 108-136. While this small surgical change was a significant improvement to the Endangered Species Act (ESA), many members of Congress are scared to death they will enrage the environmental community who are willing to spend millions in a political campaign to punish anyone who dares to change the law.

This is not mere speculation. In 2006, dishonest environmental groups like Defenders of Wildlife and the Sierra Club spent about $5 million to ruin the reputation and career of Congressman Richard Pombo of California. His crimes were being Chairman of the House Natural Resources Committee and having the guts to propose a long overdue modernization of the Endangered Species Act. Gone are the days when ESA legislation is approved with little debate and no opposition.

In the past 10 years, the House of Representatives has approved two measures to modernize the Endangered Species Act. These were the Threatened and Endangered Species Recovery Act of 2005 and the 21st Century Endangered Species Transparency Act of 2014. Both of these measures were hotly debated and passed without the support of Democrat members.

During consideration of the second measure, Natural Resources Committee Chairman and the sponsor of the proposal, Doc Hastings (R-WA) noted, "It is four sections that aim to increase transparency; to enlist greater consultation by States, localities, and tribes; and to reduce taxpayer funded attorneys' fees to help invest more funding in actual recovery." Don Young voted in favor of both pieces of legislation.

During his career in the House of Representatives, Don Young has introduced a number of bills to improve ESA. These included allowing states a larger role in the recovery of species; requiring an analysis of the economic, social, and other effects of listing; annual review of all species; enhance propagation of endangered species; greater transparency; harmonize ESA with CITES; improve science integrity; incentives for private land owners; limit citizen suits to those directly impacted by a listing decision; peer review all scientific data; relocate listed species; and transfer sole ESA authority to the U.S. Fish and Wildlife Service.

These are commonsense changes that should have been adopted because they would have improved the law. In addition, Don Young has proposed species conservation measures that have been enacted into law. He is the original author of the Neotropical Migratory Bird Conservation Act of 2000 and he has led a two-decade crusade to ensure African and Asian elephants, rhinoceros, and tigers receive a small amount of federal funding to save them in the future. Over the past decade, these four species have received about $80 million to fund 1072 projects in Asia and Africa. Without this critical investment, there is no question that wild elephants, rhinos, and tigers would be teetering on the edge of extinction.

It is now over 50 years since President Lyndon B. Johnson signed the Endangered Species Preservation Act into law. In 1966, there were 78 species awarded special protection. Today, there are 2,327 animals and plants listed as either threatened or endangered. Of this total, 1,653 are domestic species and 674 reside outside of the United States.

Hawaii has the largest number of listed species at 500. Vermont has the fewest with five listings. Alaska has 12 species that require protection. Among these species are the Eskimo curlew, Northern Sea Otter, Polar bear, and Wood Bison. There are also 30 domestic species that are candidates for listing. These include the fatmucket, Frisco clover, rattlesnake master borer moth, and the Smooth Pimpleback.

There are other species like the Eastern Diamondback Rattlesnake whose listing status is under review. This animal, which is the largest rattlesnake species, is found in Alabama, Florida, Georgia, Mississippi, North Carolina, and South Carolina. According to the Audubon Society, "This species has the reputation of being the most dangerous venomous snake in North America."

If it gains Endangered Species Act protection, then it will be unlawful to kill an Eastern Diamondback Rattlesnake or destroy its habitat. Those who violate these protections are subject to fines and imprisonment. Sadly, those Americans living in the affected six southern states will not be afforded any protections from this predator.

For those of us who have monitored the Endangered Species Act for the past 40 years, there are several simple truths. I can categorically state that those members who voted for the original law never envisioned protecting this rattlesnake or any dangerous animal. I often tell folks that if

Tyrannosaurs lived today, the Endangered Species Act would protect it.

Having said that, we must all remember that the fundamental goal of this law was not to simply list species but to recover and remove them from protection under the Act. The U.S. Fish and Wildlife Service and the National Marine Fisheries Service have approved 1158 species recovery plans. They have dedicated critical habitat for 704 species. Sadly, only 34 domestic species have been delisted.

For this handful of species, the Act has been a success. Every American should rejoice that many of our iconic species have been saved from extinction. These include Bald eagles, California condors, Peregrine Falcons, Whooping cranes, and Grizzly bears.

No one should be pleased, however, that only 34 out of 1,653 listed species have been declared recovered. This represents a recovery rate of only two percent. This is a pitifully low level and I submit if a doctor had this level of success in treating their patients they would not be practicing medicine and a lawyer with a two percent success rate is wanting for clients. Greater emphasis and resources must be allocated for recovery and not just adding a seemingly endless number of species to a critical care list with little, if any, hope of recovery.

Sadly, this will be difficult. The Endangered Species Act has become, like abortion and gun control, the third rail of politics. Despite the fact that every iteration and change to the law has been overwhelmingly adopted, there are millions of Americans, whose lives have been negatively impacted by the enforcement of this powerful environmental law.

During my career on Capitol Hill, I heard dozens of horrors stories from private landowners in the United States. Among the most famous was the California farmer who was charged with killing five kangaroo rats; the $470 million dollar earthquake proof hospital in Riverside, California that had to be moved because it was located on critical habitat for the Delhi Sands Flower Loving Fly, and Texas foresters who prematurely harvested their cedar trees to avoid them becoming critical habitat for the Golden Cheeked Warbler.

In recent years, the Congress has debated legislation to assist California farmers who have struggled with a terrible man made drought. In an effort to save a two-inch fish known as the Delta Smelt, the Obama Administration caused the loss of hundreds of thousands of acres of productive farmland and tens of thousands of jobs in Central Valley, California. The government's solution to help the Delta Smelt was to divert millions of gallons of water from the Central Valley by dumping it into the Pacific Ocean.

While former Secretary of the Interior Bruce Babbitt once testified that we as a nation had a moral obligation to save all of God's creatures, even he did not practice what he preached. In May of 1995, the U.S. Fish and Wildlife Service began a $100,000 program to eliminate sea gulls from the Monomoy National Wildlife Refuge in Massachusetts. These gulls were destroying the eggs of the threatened Piping plover and Roseate terns that lived on the refuge.

In an effort to eliminate this threat to these two-listed species, about 6,000 gulls were fed bread contaminated with the avian poison DRC-1339. The expectation was they would ingest the bread, return to their nests, and die quietly. For the wealthy residents of Chatham, Massachusetts, they were not amused when dying gulls fell out of the sky and landed on their luxury cars, in their crystal-clear pools, and on their manicured lawns. They demanded the program be stopped immediately and it was.

I am also aware that the Clinton Administration was not pleased that this controversy was the subject of a public hearing before my Subcommittee on Fisheries, Wildlife, and Oceans on July 8, 1996. A careful reading of the debate on the 1973 law makes it clear that the original sponsors of ESA never envisioned trying to save every species on the planet.

After failing to pass comprehensive legislation to improve, modernize, and reform ESA, it is time to listen to the suggestions of one of its original sponsors, Don Young. He is one of two members still serving who voted for the original 1973 law and each modification in 1978, 1979, 1982, 1998, and 2004.

The Act can be improved if the Congress requires better science, enhances state authority, greater transparency, incentives for private property owners, peer review of all listing decisions, and the removal of foreign species. There is no reason to continue to list the 674 foreign species on our ESA. They are more than adequately protected by the Convention on International Trade in Endangered Species of Wild Fauna and Flora.

If these changes are a bridge too far, then the 115th Congress should adopt legislation with two simple modifications to the Endangered Species Act. The first change would be to eliminate the mandatory establishment of critical habitat for a listed species. Under current law, critical habitat is set-aside either upon listing or no later than one year. Tens of millions of acres, including vast amounts of private property, have already been federally designated. It is fair to ask, what is the value of these designated lands?

On April 22, 1999, then Secretary of Interior Bruce Babbitt told the Senate Environment and Public Works Committee, "I have voiced my concerns about the way that we are mandated to use the designation of critical habitat under the Endangered Species Act. It does not produce good results." Just one month later, then Director of the U.S. Fish and Wildlife Service told the same Senate Committee, "In 25 years of implementing the ESA, we have found that designation of critical habitat provided little additional protection to most listed species, while it consumes significant amounts of scarce conservation resources."

These two public servants were not fans of the property development community. They worked in the Clinton Administration. They were heroes to environmentalists throughout the United States. Jamie Clark joined the Defenders of Wildlife in 2004 and seven years later was named President and CEO. This group has filed hundreds of lawsuits against the U.S. Fish and Wildlife and have advocated for the listing of thousands of plants and animals.

What Bruce Babbitt and Jamie Clark had in common was the courage to tell the U.S. Senate that the designation of critical habitat was not only counterproductive but was a magnet for lawsuits.

ESA should also be amended to change the requirement that each listed species shall be reviewed every five years. This review requirement should be discretionary and not mandatory. Together with critical habitat designation, these two features alone have resulted in hundreds of lawsuits and the diversion of badly needed funds to respond to these court actions.

These are easy cases to win in court. If the U.S. Fish and Wildlife Service fails to complete a mandatory 5-year species review or does not designate critical habitat for the Alabama beach mouse, Tooth Cave Spider, or Texas Blind Salamander, then a federal judge has no choice to rule against the agency. The net effect of the ruling is the federal agency must spend taxpayer money to defend itself, the amount of critical habitat is frequently increased, and those suing are compensated under the Equal Access to Justice Act. Sadly, the law has created a cottage industry benefiting lawyers and environmental groups and not imperiled species.

In the final analysis, the goal of ESA has always been to recover and not just list species. By repeatedly suing the federal government, the environmental community has repeatedly demonstrated they are not interested in species recovery but in publicity and filling their own financial coffers. By approving these two changes, the law will be improved and the emphasis will return to the recovery of those species that face the prospect of extinction.

This will restore the fundamental reason why Don Young voted for this Act in 1973. It will also help to validate the remarks of the former host of *The Living Planet,* Sir David Attenborough that the Endangered Species Act was, "A courageous national statement that Americans care about the magnificent land and its wealth of living resources."

CHAPTER 3: AMERICA'S FISH

As I was growing up on the eastern end of Long Island, one of my favorite pastimes was to fish. I would get my bamboo pole, bucket of hand dug worms, a few cheap hooks, and walk to the freshwater pond behind our house in Water Mill, New York. Here I would spend hours enjoying the tranquility of that peaceful place.

I would also spend time reading some of the classics. Among those I admired most was Ernest Hemingway's masterpiece *The Old Man and The Sea*. I empathized with the struggles of Santiago, the aging Cuban fisherman, who hooks a giant marlin but ultimately loses his fish to hungry mako sharks. In this wonderful novel, Hemingway writes, "You are killing me, fish, the old man thought. But you have a right to. Never have I seen a greater, or more beautiful, or calmer or more noble thing than you, brother."

For the past 400 years, international law has promoted a policy of freedom of the seas. Dutch jurist Hugo Grotius first proposed this doctrine in 1609. In his book, *The Right Which Belongs to the Dutch to Take Part in the East Indian Trade,* Grotius espoused the doctrine that the high seas should be open to all nations in times of peace.

While most Americans are familiar with the role Captain John Smith played in the founding of Jamestown, Virginia, much less is known about his commercial fishing exploits. Yet, he was a successful fisherman who returned to Europe in 1614 with, "Seven thousand 'green cod' or salted fish, and forty thousand stock fish, or 'dried cod,' which his men had landed off of Monhegan Island in Southern Maine."

Fishing has always been woven in the fabric of this country. It has been an integral part of Don Young's life. As an avid fisherman, guide, and licensed mariner, he has spent a lifetime enjoying Alaska's bountiful fishery resources. He is one of our most prominent conservationists who is committed to protecting our renewable resources.

Commercial fishing has played a vital role in the livelihoods of millions of Americans. These folks live in cities like Dutch Harbor, Gloucester, Kodiak, Nantucket, New Bedford, Seattle, and Seward. They catch cod, halibut, mackerel, Pollock, and salmon.

On September 28, 1945, President Harry S. Truman issued Proclamation 2667. This document established our nation's policy as it affected the subsoil and seabed of the Outer Continental Shelf (OCS). It declared for the first time that the United States would control waters up to 200-miles off our shores. U.S. geologists had determined that vast amounts of gas, minerals, and oil likely existed on the OCS.

President Truman wanted Americans to control and utilize those valuable natural resources. This policy was codified in the enactment of the Outer Continental Shelf Lands Act of 1953.

While this Executive Order did not affect commercial fishing, this oversight was remedied the same day. In Proclamation 2668, President Truman declared that, "There is an urgent need to protect coastal fishery resources from destructive exploitation." His solution was to, "Establish conservation zones in those areas of the high seas contiguous to the coasts of the United States wherein fishing activities have been or in the future may be developed and maintained on a substantive scale." The fundamental reason for the Proclamation, which was never implemented into law, was the Japanese fishermen's incursion into the Alaska Bristol Bay Red Salmon fishery.

As a consequence of these Proclamations, three Latin American countries, Chile, Peru, and Ecuador extended their own sovereign rights to 200 nautical miles off their coasts. This designation prohibited foreign fishing in the resource rich Humbolt Current System. Only Jordan and Palau use a three-mile coastal limit.

Throughout the years, various techniques have been used to successfully catch fish. These include: dredges, gill nets, hand lines, hooks, long lines, nets, pots, purse seines, and traps. In 1938, U.S. fishermen landed 4.3 billion pounds of fish. Twenty years later, our fishermen took 90 percent of the total catch off the Atlantic Coast. At the same time, 104 U.S. boats were catching 11 million pounds of halibut off the coast of Alaska.

In the early 1970's, there were about 150,000 U.S. commercial fishermen, 2,000 importers and exporters, 1,800 processors, 1,200 wholesalers, and 85,000 businesses utilizing fish products. To catch fish, men and women were willing to work in the most dangerous job in America. In the 1980's and 1990's, crab and halibut fishing were two of the most dangerous occupations in the United States. Between 1980 and 1988, an average of 31 fishermen died in Alaska each year. The primary reasons for these deaths were overloaded boats, exhausted crews, and inflexibly short fishing seasons. Boats were fishing in terrible weather conditions to catch the allotted quota before the season closed.

While fishing is still a dangerous job, no one lost their life in Alaska in 2015, despite the sinking of six commercial fishing boats. According to Coast Guard Spokesman Scott Wilwert, "Management practices have made fishing safer --- the end of the famous derby-style halibut and crab fisheries in particular. Fishermen are better equipped and better prepared." I would add that crab rationalization and fishing quotas (IFQ's) have made fishing seasons not only longer but also safer.

They have allowed captains much more flexibility in deciding when and where they will fish.

As someone who has watched the development of federal fishing legislation for the past 20 years, I can unequivocally attest that these conservation and safety measures would not have been implemented without the tireless leadership of Don Young. His efforts have saved countless lives.

While in 1953, U.S. fishermen had exclusive control over the Bering Sea and the Georges Bank off of New England, the industry was about to radically change when the first stern trawler was constructed in Aberdeen, Scotland. This ship, the *Fairtry,* was 200 feet long and 2,600 gross tons.

A factory trawler is a boat that catches fish by pulling through the water a net shaped like an open mouthed bag. It also has the ability to process and freeze the fish. What this meant was that a vessel no longer had to immediately return to port. It could stay at sea for an almost an indefinite period of time while it caught, processed, and froze millions of pounds of fish. Their only limitations are the size of its freezer and whether a huge mother ship was in the region. In the commercial fishing industry, a mother ship is a large ocean going vessel that processes and freezes fish caught by smaller ships.

As you might expect, hundreds of factory stern trawlers were built in Scotland and West Germany. They were flagged by the nations of Bulgaria, China, Cuba, Italy, Japan, Poland, Romania, Spain, and the Union of Soviet Socialists Republics (USSR). These giant factory trawlers took up residence off the coast of New England and in the Bering Sea.

By 1974, there were thousands of foreign flagged factory trawlers fishing on the Canadian Grand Banks and the waters off of New England. The Russians alone had 710 factory trawlers and 103 factory mother ships to process the fish caught between Greenland and New England. It took more than a 100 years between 1647 and 1750 for North American fishermen to harvest 8 million tons of cod. It took foreign factory trawlers just 15 years to catch the same amount of fish.

While the U.S. did not have a factory trawler until 1983, America was largely responsible for rebuilding Western Europe and Japan after the end of the Second World War. Under the leadership of Secretary of State George C. Marshall, the Congress enacted the Economic Cooperation Act of 1948. This legislation appropriated $13.3 billion that was allocated to 16 European countries to rebuild their economies. West Germany received $1.3 billion or 11 percent of the total allocation.

Although Japan did not receive any Marshall Plan money, our government did send $2.4 billion between 1945 and 1953. The Supreme Commander for Allied Forces General Douglas MacArthur oversaw the successful occupation and rebuilding of postwar Japan including its fishing and shipbuilding sectors.

In the case of Japan and West Germany much of its infrastructure was destroyed in the war. As the architect of the recovery plan, Secretary Marshall strongly believed that, "It is logical that the United States should do whatever it is able to do to assist in the return of normal economic health in the world." As a result, U.S. taxpayer money was used to rebuild their factories, including their shipyards. While both of these countries have been allies for over 70 years, the unintended consequence of our generosity was that these rebuilt factories produced a fleet of factory trawlers that destroyed a significant portion of the U.S. commercial fishing industry.

Pulitzer prize winning author, William W. Warner wrote in his 1983 book *Distant Waters*, "Try to imagine a mobile and completely self-contained timber-cutting machine that could smash through the roughest trails of the forest, cut down trees, mill them, and deliver consumer ready lumber in half the time of normal logging and milling operations. This is exactly what factory trawlers did --- this was exactly their effect on fish --- in the forests of the deep. It could not long go unnoticed."

Their impact on fishery resources was catastrophic. By 1972, the U.S. fishery share had fallen from 92 percent to 49 percent, imports of fish products tripled to 5.5 billion pounds, and the U.S. trade imbalance significantly rose to $1.3 billion dollars. This was a 318 percent increase from 1960. In the Bering Sea, the seven surviving U.S. halibut boats caught 167,000 pounds of that fish. Japanese fishermen caught 11 million pounds of our halibut.

In New England, the total catch fell from 591 million pounds to 248 million, U.S. fishermen caught only 10.4 percent in the Georges Bank, and ships flying the flag of the USSR watched their share increase from 68,000 pounds in 1961 to 1 million pounds a decade later. This was a fascinating development because the Russians did not have an ocean fishery until 1945.

In the document *The Postwar Expansion of Russia's Fishing Industry,* the Fisheries Research Institute at the University of Washington concluded in January 1964 that, "Soviet fishing almost doubled in a decade and in 1960, the U.S.S.R. replaced the U.S. as the world's fourth largest fishing nation, behind Japan, Peru, and Communist China." This report, which had been prepared for the Senate Commerce Committee, lead its Chairman, Senator Warren Magnuson, to suggest that, "Fisheries are one of the major battlefields in the Cold War." Chairman Magnuson was not only correct but sadly our federal government, especially the U.S. State Department, did nothing to stop the Russians from destroying our commercial fishing industry. This unsustainable harvest of cod, haddock, hake, herring, and flounder led to the inevitable collapse of these fisheries.

At the same time, foreign factory trawlers were doing their best to catch the last fish in the Eastern Bering Sea. According to Greenpeace U.S.A., "By the early 1970's, indications of overfishing in the Eastern Bering Sea Pollock stocks were evident. Landings (Pollock) increased from 175,000 metric tons in 1964 to 1.9 million metric tons in 1972, most of which were caught by the Japanese fleet."

The National Marine Fisheries Service, which is charged with the responsibility of managing fishery resources commented that, "By 1975, all the major commercial species of the Bering Sea region were considered fully exploited or over-exploited including the two most abundant species --- Pollock and yellowfin sole."

By the mid-1970's, the U.S. commercial fishing industry was facing a terrible crisis. International agreements had failed miserably to prevent overfishing. The Law of the Sea Treaty was being debated interminably and our most valuable fishery stocks were being decimated. Our fishermen could not compete with foreign factory trawlers and fishing communities were dying.

Those living in those communities demanded immediate action from the United States Congress. They were not going to sit idly by as their fish, livelihoods, and way of life was being destroyed. In a sense, they were supporting an American First Policy to protect our fish from the Italians, Japanese, Russians, Spaniards, and West Germans who were exploiting them.

To make matters worse, foreign factory trawlers were harvesting our fish and then selling them back to U.S. consumers. In 1975, foreign fishermen caught $500 million dollars of our bottom fisheries off the coast of Alaska and we imported half of that total. This was an insane policy.

In response to this outcry, the House of Representatives passed House Concurrent Resolution 173 on December 4, 1973. Congressmen David Treen (R-LA) and Don Young sponsored it. This Resolution stated that, "It is the policy of the Congress that our fishing industry be afforded all support necessary to have it strengthened, and all steps be taken to provide adequate protection for our coastal fisheries against excessive foreign fishing."

According to its author, David Treen, "This Resolution is our declaration of purpose, and that purpose is for the Congress of the United States to direct its attention more intensely and more seriously to the problems of the American fishing industry." The bill was approved unanimously on a 405 to 0 vote. It was the first legislative step to end the stranglehold of foreign fishermen.

During the same 93rd Congress, the U.S. Senate approved S. 1988, the Interim Fisheries Zone Extension and Management Act on December 11, 1974. This bill sponsored by Senators Warren G. Magnuson and Ted Stevens established a temporary 200-mile zone for the United States. This designation would automatically terminate when the Law of the Sea Treaty came into force. While the United States signed this agreement in 1994, the U.S. Senate has still not ratified the Law of the Sea Treaty and we are not a party to that Convention.

In the 94th Congress, the bipartisan leadership of Congressmen Gerry E. Studds of Massachusetts and Don Young of Alaska introduced H. R. 200, the Interim Fisheries Zone Extension and Management Act. While Gerry Studds was a liberal and Don Young a conservative, both of these outstanding legislators represented fishing communities and they were committed to saving the U.S. commercial fishing industry. Senators Warren Magnuson and

Ted Stevens introduced a Senate companion bill, S. 961.

There were nearly 40 days of hearings on the issue of extending the United States Exclusive Fishery Zone from 12 to 200 miles over a three-year period. Four of those hearings were held in Kodiak, Sitka, and Juneau, Alaska. At a public hearing at the Federal Building in Juneau, Chairman Ted Stevens opined, "The seriousness of foreign devastation of our fish stocks seems to be gaining much more attention than in the past. It has taken a long time for our fishermen to be heard, and the situation is so dangerous now that we must do everything possible to see that something is done." He also vividly described how, "Foreign fleets harvest the fish of North American waters just as effectively as a farmer cuts his wheat or a logger clear-cuts a forest."

Governor Jay Hammond told the Senate Commerce, Science and Transportation Committee that the State of Alaska strongly supported extending the U.S. fishery jurisdiction seaward 200 nautical miles from their coast.

At the March 10, 1975 hearing before the House Merchant Marine and Fisheries Subcommittee on Fisheries and Wildlife Conservation and the Environment, Don Young told his colleagues, "No single industry employs as many Alaskans as does the fishing industry at the height of its season. In the past decade, foreign invasion of Alaska's fishing stocks has depleted those stocks to the extent that the viability of the industry is threatened. In my estimate this hearing will consider the legislation which represents the last hope for the fisheries in my state."

Two days later, John Hall and Bart Eaton who were representing the United Fishermen's Marketing Association and Kodiak Shrimp Trawlers Association of Alaska told the same Subcommittee, "The United States has absurdly ignored the deliberate ravaging of our richest marine environment or has traded that environment away and with it, our livelihood. We fishermen are being robbed and cheated. The foreigners are plundering our coastal waters and reducing entire species of fish such as Pollock, halibut, Pacific Ocean perch, and others to extinction."

The fundamental goal of H.R. 200 was to reserve the 200 miles from our shores for the exclusive benefit of our fishermen. This was a direct result of the utter failure of international fishing agreements. The legislation also established priority rights for U.S. fishermen within the zone; created eight Regional Fishery Management Councils to develop management plans and regulations; banned seafood imports from nations refusing to grant equitable access for U.S. vessels; called for the establishment of a comprehensive management program governing U.S. and foreign fisheries; and it established penalties for all violations of the Act.

Under this bill, foreign fishing was not entirely prohibited within the 200-mile zone. However, to participate within the zone, foreign nations must sign a bilateral Governing International Fishery Agreement with the United States.

Members of the House Merchant Marine and Fisheries Committee overwhelmingly supported the Studds-Young bill. However, in the Committee's report on the legislation, Ambassador John Norton Moore writing on behalf of the Department of State noted, "We recognize that the coastal fishermen of the United States have encountered severe problems in recent years and that overfishing for some species has caused a depletion of the stocks involved. However, in our view the best solution can be attained by multinational agreements in the Third U.N. Conference on the Law of the Sea. The Executive Branch opposes the enactment of the bills (H.R. 200) discussed in this letter."

Nearly two months later, the House considered H.R. 200 on October 9, 1975. In his opening statement, Gerry Studds noted, "Since I first introduced the bill in June of 1973, the House Merchant Marine and Fisheries Committee has held almost continuous hearings on the bill and the need for urgent conservation measures to prevent destruction of our marine fisheries."

Don Young told his House colleagues; "Today is a great day in American history and a great day for the State of Alaska because we are going to enact a piece of legislation which is long overdue. What we are saying in this bill is that it is time for Americans to speak up for Americans to take care of renewal resources that are along our coasts, otherwise these foreign vessels would not be 12 miles off."

Don Young is a master of educating his colleagues through the use of show-and-tell items like leg-hold traps, monofilament nets, or an oosik. He went on to tell the audience in the House of Representatives that, "The Members may wonder why I have brought this box into the Chamber. It contains a net, which the Japanese utilize, to catch our salmon in a way that every one of our scientists and biologists say we should not follow. It is a net made of monofilament. It never destroys itself. It is a 2-inch mesh, and this one net alone, when found upon the beach after it had been cut loose, contained one caribou, numerous ducks, and over 100 salmon of all sizes."

He concluded his remarks by reciting the first verse of Alaska's Flag Song. Marie Drake, a long-time employee of Alaska's Department of Education, wrote this composition. It became the official State Song in 1955. The lyrics are:

Eight stars of gold on a field of blue,
Alaska's flag, may it mean to you,
The blue of the sea, the evening sky,
The mountain lakes and the flowers nearby, The gold of the early sourdough's dreams, The precious gold of the hills and streams, The brilliant stars in the northern sky,
The "Bear", the "Dipper," and shining high,
The great North Star with its steady light, O'er land and sea a beacon bright,
Alaska's flag to Alaskans dear,
The simple flag of a last frontier.

Finally, the House Majority Leader Thomas "Tip" O'Neill (D-MA) stated, "But Congress can not stand back and watch the depletion of our fisheries resources forever. When it became clear that the latest session of the Law of the Sea Conference would not successfully contend with the problems in this area, it became incumbent on Congress to act expeditiously."

At the conclusion of debate, the House voted 208 to 101 to approve H.R. 200. Remarkably, 123 members choose not to vote on this measure. The primary reasons why 83 Democrats and 40 Republicans choose not to cast a Yea or Nay vote, were; it had been a long debate on the legislation, many amendments had been offered, it was late in the evening, it was the last vote of the day, and it was getaway day with Members not returning for almost two weeks. There was frantic rush to the nearest airport.

On January 28, 1976, the U.S. Senate debated S. 961, the Emergency Marine Fisheries Protection Act. As a co-sponsor, Ted Stevens stated that, "I believe this bill will allow Alaskans to make a more significant contribution to the nation than all the oil or gas or minerals that we discover and produce in our State. This is an action which is absolutely essential to assure that solid conservation and management principles apply to the renewal resources of our seas."

At the conclusion of the debate, the Senate adopted the House version, H.R. 200 by a vote of 77 to 19. Ironically, one of the Nay votes was the Junior Senator from Alaska, Mike Gravel. In his statement, Senator Gravel noted, "If the proponents of the bill are true and wish conservation, they can get it through Article 7 of the Geneva Convention. But I submit that is not what they want. They want unilateral, total control 200-mile ribbon around this nation so that they can exclude all foreign fishing. I submit that will not be morally tolerated by this great nation of ours nor will it be tolerated in the world today."

After successfully passing both the House of Representatives and the U.S. Senate by overwhelmingly margins, members of both bodies resolved their various differences. On March 30, 1976, the House debated the Conference Report on H.R. 200, which was now called the Fishery Conservation and Management Act. At that time, co-author Don Young stated, "As we look at this legislation it does affect the State of Alaska because of the great area of Alaska touching on the Bering Sea. This legislation is long overdue. It is time that we wake up to reality. We must see to it that this nation of ours is protected in this vital area and that is what this bill does." The Conference Report was approved in the House on a vote of 346 to 52 and by unanimous consent in the Senate.

What was sent to the White House was legislation that had the purpose of conserving and managing those resources within the Exclusive Fishery Conservation Zone for all fish except highly migratory species like billfish, swordfish, and tuna. This was accomplished by: establishing a 200-mile fishery conservation zone as of March 1, 1977; prohibited foreign fishing after February 28, 1977; established procedures for international fishery agreements; creating a National Fishery Management Program including national standards or guiding conservation principles; establishing eight Regional Fishery Management Councils; and improvements to the Atlantic Tunas Convention Act of 1975 and the Fishermen's Protective Act of 1967.

On April 13, 1976, President Gerald R. Ford signed H.R. 200, the Fishery Conservation and Management Act into law, despite the objections of his own State Department. It became Public Law 94-265. In a signing statement, President Ford said, "The extension of our jurisdiction to 200 miles will enable us to protect and conserve the valuable fisheries off our coasts. The foreign overfishing off our coasts cannot be allowed to continue without resolution. In the absence of a timely treaty, no nation can be assured that its paramount interest in the oceans will be protected." It is not often that the U.S. Congress enacts a bill designed to save an entire industry.

It is now more than 40 years since the United States established a 200-mile exclusive zone. While it may have started out as a temporary designation, it has become a permanent feature of federal law. In fact, on March 10, 1983, President Ronald W. Reagan issued Proclamation 5030 entitled *Exclusive Economic Zone of the United States.* This further memorialized the U.S. policies over the continental shelf, fisheries, and marine mammals. I am also not aware of any executive, judicial, or legislative effort to reinstate a 12-mile zone.

With all due respect to former Senator Gravel, U.S. fishermen would likely still be waiting for help from the Geneva Convention or the United Nations, had H.R. 200, the Studds-Young bill not be enacted into law. And it would have been immoral to allow fishing families in Alaska, California, Louisiana, Massachusetts, Texas, and Washington State to be destroyed by foreign nations catching our fish.

While sadly cod and other ground fisheries remain depleted in the Georges Bank, fishery resources in the Bering Sea and North Pacific are healthy, sustainable and highly profitable. The Alaskan Pollock fishery has become a billion dollar industry with more than 3 million tons being caught each year. This represents the second most important fish species in terms of total catch.

Alaskan Pollock are a fast growing and short-lived species. It is a member of the cod family Gadidae. Due to its mild taste and whiter color, it is used to make Filet-O-Fish sandwiches for MacDonald's, fish taco's at Long John Silver's, fish sticks for our public school cafeterias, imitation crabmeat for our salads, and surimi that is a paste used in a variety of Asian foods. More importantly, this fishery is vibrant because of the tireless conservation efforts of Don Young and the North Pacific Regional Fishery Management Council.

The Fishery Conservation and Management Act, which is now known as the Magnuson-Stevens Act, has achieved its goal of eliminating foreign fishing in the U.S. Exclusive Economic Zone. The percentage of fish harvest by foreign countries has significantly declined from 71 percent of the total catch in 1977 to zero percent in 1991. Foreign vessels harvested a small quantity of Atlantic herring in 2001.

I also find it remarkable that in just three short years, Don Young was in the leadership forefront in passing the Trans-Alaskan Pipeline Act of 1973, the Endangered Species Act of 1973, and the Fishery Conservation and Management Act of 1976. These three federal laws are landmark statutes. Most Members of Congress would be thrilled to make a major contribution to even one such important law.

Don Young was a key player in each of these three huge legislative achievements and he was just getting started. As Don Young has frequently told the nation, "Today is a Great Day for the State of Alaska!"

CHAPTER 4: ALASKA'S LANDS

The Merriam-Webster dictionary defines the word obsession as "a persistent disturbing preoccupation with an unreasonable idea." For the past century, the U.S. federal government has been obsessed with acquiring and controlling vast amounts of public land.

As evidence of this policy, you need only examine the four western states of Alaska, Idaho, Nevada, and Utah. The U.S. government owns more than 60 percent of each state with the highest concentration of 85 percent being located in the Silver State. This represents 379 million acres of land. By contrast, the federal government holds only 9 million acres in the original 13 states.

For more than 90 years, the federal government had an iron grip on almost all of the 375 million acres of Alaska. Upon becoming a state in 1959, less than one million acres were held by private citizens. Significant portions of those lands were acquired under the Homestead Act of 1962. Under this federal law, any man over the age of 21 years old was eligible to stake out 160 acres of land in Alaska. In return, they were required to live on the land, build a residence, and farm at least 10 percent of the property.

What this meant was that all decisions affecting energy development, hunting, fishing, mineral exploration, and timber harvesting were made not in Alaska but in Washington, D.C. As a result, development within the state was impeded causing the loss of thousands of potential jobs and millions of dollars of tax revenue.

With the enactment of the Statehood Act, Alaska was authorized to select 104.5 million acres. This was the first of three major federal laws that determined how land would be owned, maintained, and utilized in the future. President Richard M. Nixon signed the second statute, the Alaska Native Claims Settlement Act (ANCSA), into law on December 31, 1971. This legislation was necessary because the Federal Bureau of Land Management had been awarding to the State of Alaska certain lands without taking into account or even informing native Alaskan groups.

Section 2 of Public Law 92-203 states, "Congress finds and declares that there is an immediate need for a fair and just settlement of all claims by natives and native groups of Alaska, based on aboriginal land claims." Under the law, 80,000 Alaskan natives were authorized to select and receive title to 44 million acres of public land in Alaska. The 12 Alaskan Native Regional Corporations and 225 village corporations administered the selection of these lands. It was the largest land claims settlement in U.S. history.

This law also paid Alaskan natives $962 million to extinguish their aboriginal land claims. This money was deposited into the Alaska Native Fund. Of this total amount, the Congress appropriated $462 million and the remaining $500 million was provided by the State of Alaska and from federal oil and gas leases.

While the fundamental goal of settling the aboriginal land claims of Alaskan natives had been achieved, this didn't prevent the authors of ANCSA from adding extraneous provisions to the law. The most consequential was Section 17 (d) (2).

Specifically, it directed the Secretary of the Interior to withdraw "up to, but not to exceed, 80 million acres of unreserved public lands in the State of Alaska, including previously classified lands, which the Secretary deems are suitable for addition to or creation as units of the national park, forest, wildlife refuge, and wild and scenic rivers systems." Why was this section necessary? It had absolutely nothing to do with resolving claims or fairly compensating Alaskan natives. It was added by Members of Congress who believed only the federal government should decide how public lands in Alaska will be managed.

This section also established a ten member joint Federal-State Planning Commission for Alaska. This Commission's charge was, "undertake a process of land-use planning, including the identification of and the recommendations concerning areas planned and best suited for permanent reservation in federal ownerships as parks, game refuges, and other public uses." The Commission was directed to submit its final report to the President, the Congress, the Governor of Alaska, and the Alaska state legislature no later than May 30, 1976.

On December 17, 1972, less than a year after the enactment of ANCSA and four years before the Joint Commission's final report deadline, then Secretary of Interior Rogers C.B. Morton sent to the Congress a plan to select not 80 but 127 million acres of (d) (2) lands. This set in motion the third and final law to classify lands in Alaska.

The reaction from Alaska was immediate. Alaskan Attorney General John E. Havelock called the plan a "sell out of the people of Alaska." Congressman Nick Begich described it as a "massive land grab" and even the state's liberal newspaper the *Anchorage Times* called it, "a dirty deed."

In Washington, Florida Congressman James A. Haley (D-FL), whose district was 4,800 miles from Anchorage, introduced the Morton proposal in the House of Representatives. For the next six years, this and many similar proposals were largely ignored.

Sadly, the political landscape changed in May of 1978. At that time, the House of Representatives approved H.R. 39, the Alaska National Interest Lands Conservation Act. Congressman Morris K. Udall (D-AZ) had sponsored the measure. During the bill's consideration, Don Young successfully offered 80 amendments to the legislation.

Upon its passage, the bill was referred to the Senate Committee on Energy and Natural Resources. During Senate Committee consideration, Alaskan Senator Ted Stevens successfully offered a number of significant changes to the bill. These modifications were unacceptable to the Carter Administration and the Democrats who sponsored the bill in the House.

Throughout the history of the State of Alaska, it was not a coincidence that Alaskan land bills were introduced not by the state's duly elected representatives but primarily by liberal politicians from states like Arizona, California, Florida, Ohio, and Minnesota. It also was sheer chutzpah for out of state members to reject the recommendations of Alaska's Senior Senator who was trying to improve an Alaskan land bill for his constituents.

What I witnessed during my long Congressional career, were Members of Congress, who had the misplaced notion that they could better represent the citizens of Alaska. This paternalistic attitude was ill conceived, repugnant, and wrong. These members were elected to represent their own constituents and not Alaska. If they wanted to represent the 49ᵗʰ State, they should have resigned from office, moved to Alaska, establish state residency, and then run for political office. In the meantime, they should have minded their own constituent's business. Among the leaders of this misguided group were Congressmen Morris K. Udall, Phil Burton (D-CA), John F. Seiberling (D-OH), and Bruce Vento (D-MN).

With the sunset for (d) (2) land selections expiring on December 18, 1978, the House approved legislation to extend the deadline for these selections for an additional year. When the Senate tried to consider this proposal, Alaskan Senator Mike Gravel threatened to filibuster. Senator Majority Leader Robert Byrd (D-WV) apparently felt he did not have the necessary 60 votes to stop a filibuster and the 95ᵗʰ Congress adjourned without voting on the one-year extension.

On December 1, 1978, President Jimmy Carter retaliated by using the Antiquities Act of 1906 to designate 15 national monuments in Alaska. These monuments affected 56 million acres, which was larger than 40 U.S. states. This action was universally condemned in Alaska. President Carter was burned in effigy in Fairbanks. Don Young loudly complained, "Alaskans have been slanderously portrayed as land rapists by the preservation lobby and the President has chosen to believe this image."

Congressman John Lacey (R-IO) had originally sponsored the Antiquities Act. Its goal was to authorize the President, "To declare by public proclamation historic landmarks, historic and prehistoric structures, and other objects of historic or scientific interest." President Theodore Roosevelt signed the Antiquities Act into law on June 8, 1906.

President Roosevelt was fond of the authority provided to him in Public Law 59-209. During his almost eight years in office, he designated 18 "historic sites" comprised of 1.5 million acres. Among the famous monuments were the Grand Canyon National Park in Arizona, the Muir Woods National Monument in California, and the Natural Bridges National Monument in Utah.

In the 101 years since its enactment, 15 Presidents have designated 154 sites with 843 million acres being protected for conservation. By political party, Democrat Presidents have designated 88 monuments with 620 million acres. Republican Presidents have established 66 monuments within 223 million acres. The leader in terms of both number and acreage was President Barack Obama. During his eight years, he designated a stunning 26 monuments with more than 550 million acres.

Unlike President Theodore Roosevelt, I am not a fan of the Antiquities Act. Like most federal laws, its initial application was modest. Since 1992, however, there has been a growing abuse of this powerful Presidential authority. From 1992 to 2016, Presidents William Clinton, George W. Bush, and Barack Obama have established 51 historic sites or one-third of the total. In terms of acreage, these three Administrations designated 778 million acres that is 92 percent of those lands selected since 1906.

The process to establish national monuments by Executive Orders is undemocratic. It requires an Act of Congress to add one acre of land to a national forest, national park, or wilderness area. Yet, a President can designate a 100 million acre national monument without any public hearings, any questioning of witnesses, any public examinations of the merits of such a designation, and any opportunity for elected representatives to vote up or down.

In his December 1, 1978 announcement, President Carter justified his designation of 15 national monuments in Alaska. In his statement, he stated, "Because of the risks of immediate damage to these magnificent areas, I felt it was imperative to protect all these lands and preserve for the Congress an unhampered opportunity to act next year."

I found this statement remarkably misleading. None of the 56 million acres were in any danger of immediate damage. The federal government controlled them. And, the word "unhampered" is inaccurate. If the Congress had chosen to do nothing, those lands would have remained national monuments.

Nevertheless, because of this designation, there was a renewed effort to enact an Alaska lands bill when the 96ᵗʰ Congress convened on January 3, 1979. On that day, Morris Udall, who was the Chairman of the House Interior and Insular Affairs Committee, proposed a new more comprehensive and restrictive version of the Alaska National Lands Interest Conservation Act. The bill was jointly referred to the Interior and Insular Affairs and the Merchant Marine and Fisheries Committees.

Don Young was a member of both Committees and was, therefore, uniquely positioned to play a major leadership role in the crafting of this legislation. Throughout his Congressional career, Don Young has prided himself on his commitment to all of the people of Alaska. He has embraced the notion of tirelessly representing each of the diverse groups that reside within the 49ᵗʰ State. I am sure he would agree with the views of Winston Churchill that, "It is the people who control the government, not the government the people."

In the 96th Congress, the two relevant Committees conducted nine days of public hearings including a marathon 13-hour session held at the University of Alaska at Fairbanks. On March 10, 1979, nine members of the House Subcommittee on Fisheries and Wildlife Conservation and the Environment traveled to Alaska in the middle of the winter to hear testimony from 78 witnesses representing state officials, Mayors, native Alaskans, trappers, lodge owners, the hunting and conservation community, environmentalists, and Alaskans representing their communities or themselves.

As the hearing began, the host Don Young noted, "As emotional as we wish it to be, the facts are what is going to impress these colleagues of mine. This is a Chairman (John Breaux) who has vision and wisdom, and this is a Committee that I believe will do the job that is proper for the State of Alaska."

In his remarks, Alaskan Governor Jay Hammond told the Subcommittee, "It was a difficult issue to deal with, this whole subject of (d) (2), because frankly, most Alaskans were not desirous of changing the then status quo. Too often we find persons who attempt to come to Alaska to tell us what is best for us."

The Subcommittee also heard from Jack Boone who was representing the residents of Eagle, Alaska. This small town is located along the Yukon River on the U.S.-Canada border. It has a current population of 86 folks. He told the members, "We who use the land do not feel that we are committing any crime. It feeds us, clothes some of us, keeps us warm, and provides some cash for those necessities we do need from the outside world. We love it and take pretty good care of it, and consider ourselves much better conservationists, because we are informed conservationists, than people several thousand miles away."

E. R. Chipp the Vice President of the Resource Associates of Alaska did not mince words when he declared, "Economic and political war has been declared on Alaska by the Administration, and business people will not invest money in Alaska. Carter stated that he will not allow mining to take place in Alaska; Andrus stated this in numerous ways; and Udall is not satisfied with only being Lord and Master over Arizona."

Finally, as midnight approached, Chairman Breaux thanked his colleagues for traveling to Alaska, complimented Don Young for all of the hearing arrangements, and spoke these poetic words "My father told me one time that, in his opinion, the two greatest lies ever told were, First, 'I put my check in the mail this morning.' and second 'I am from the federal government and I am here to help you." The people of Alaska had already had a bellyful of help from Washington, D.C.

On April 18, 1979, the House Interior Committee met to consider and vote on the merits of H.R. 39. After a highly contentious debate, the Committee remarkably adopted an amendment offered by Congressman Jerry Huckaby, a Democrat from Shreveport, Louisiana. His amendment was approved on a vote of 22 to 21 with every Republican member, including Don Young, supporting it. It was far less restrictive than H.R. 39, as introduced, it was much more sympathetic to the State of Alaska, and it allowed energy exploration in the Coastal Plain of the Arctic National Wildlife Refuge.

It was therefore, not surprising that Chairman Udall and other leading Democrats were apoplectic at this shocking outcome. In the Committee Report on H.R. 39, which is always written by the Chairman of the jurisdictional Committee, Chairman Udall and 17 other Democrats complained that, "By a single vote, the Committee rejected the refined Udall-Seiberling bill. This Huckaby Substitute has been found flatly unacceptable, not only by us but also by the Administration." One group that did not object to the adoption of the Huckaby Substitute was the citizens of Alaska. It is a pity that Chairman Udall did not value their opinion.

It must have been a painful experience for Chairman Udall to submit his Committee Report on H.R. 39 that had the standard boilerplate language. It said, "The Committee on Interior and Insular Affairs, to whom was referred the bill H.R. 39 to provide for the designation and conservation of certain public lands in Alaska, reports favorably thereon with amendments and recommends that the bill as amended do pass."

Just five days later, the Merchant Marine and Fisheries Committee voted on its version of H.R. 39. In this case, Congressman John Breaux sponsored the approved language. This version was similar to the Huckaby Substitute with the addition of a provision allowing the Coastal Plain of the Arctic National Wildlife Refuge (ANWR) to be open for private oil and gas exploration. ANWR is our nation's largest refuge with 19 million acres. Of that total, 9 million acres, which is an area larger than the states of Connecticut, Delaware, New Jersey, and Rhode Island, is classified as wilderness.

While there are a number of wildlife refuges where mineral leasing and oil and gas development occur, to the environmental community, the Arctic National Wildlife Refuge is their Serengeti. These groups have tried for over 40 years to designate the 1.5 million acres of the Coastal Plain as wilderness.

In the Merchant Marine and Fisheries Committee report, eight liberal Democrats from Florida, Maryland, Massachusetts, New Jersey, Oregon, and

Washington State filed dissenting views. These members stated, "We object to the Breaux bill on both procedural and substantive grounds. We believe it represents a major step backwards for the national interest in conserving wildlife and wilderness on public lands in Alaska." Once again, the people of Alaska whose opinion should have been given priority did not object to the Breaux bill.

Despite the fact that the Udall bill had 152 cosponsors including 18 Republicans, the two House Committees with jurisdiction over Alaskan lands rejected their version of H.R. 39. This was a huge blow to national environmental groups who spent tens of millions of dollars urging Members of Congress to lock-up Alaska's precious natural resources. Sadly, not one of these groups told their audience that the 1002 area might contain the largest onshore oil deposits in North America.

In the House of Representatives, the Rules Committee always considers bills like H.R. 39. It is a body controlled by the Speaker of the House of Representatives who appoints 11 of the 15 members. It is the Committee's job, which it has performed since 1789, to decide how long a bill will be considered, what amendments can be debated, and who will offer them.

In the case of H.R. 39, Speaker Thomas P. O'Neill was highly sympathetic to the views of Chairman Morris Udall. As a result, the Rules Committee was instructed to approve a "Special Rule" that allowed amendments to be offered by Morris Udall, Jerry Huckaby, and John Breaux in that order. However, if the Udall Substitute was approved, then the voting outcome of the other two amendments was irrelevant. This was an unusual and undemocratic rule. In this case, preference was given to an amendment that had been rejected by not one but the two House Committees who were responsible for drafting the legislation.

On May 4, 1979, the House began its consideration of H.R. 39. In his opening statement, Chairman Udall declared, "We have to make a settlement for the 220 million people of the United States. They are entitled to have the crown jewels, the Yosemite's, the Grand Canyons of Alaska set aside for future generations." Upon completion of general debate, the Udall-Anderson amendment was offered. It was even more sweeping and restrictive than the version introduced on January 3, 1979 or the bill that passed the House in 1978. Huge amounts of oil and mineral development areas were classified as wilderness and all future economic activity within those areas was prohibited.

This prompted Don Young to state, "The Udall-Anderson bill very honestly does a great disservice to my State and to the nation as a whole. Members are being pressured now to support a bill called the

Udall-Anderson bill that has had no hearings, no public testimony, no Committee participation, and a bill which has been drawn up, frankly, in the backrooms of the two gentlemen which I have mentioned." A Committee did not consider this new version of H.R. 39 because Morris Udall understood his new backroom bill would be rejected again.

John Dingell joined the debate when he said, "I must confess that the gentleman has been so busy perfecting this that very few people in the House, including his own Committee, can keep up with it. I really think we ought to focus on a piece of legislation that has been considered by the Committee and has not gone through this rapid series of changes of remarkable distractions that permits it to grow from 149 to 335 pages."

After three days of intensive debate, tempers were short, members were tired of endless lobbying, and many Congressmen felt the politically safe position was to simply support the Udall-Anderson amendment. By taking this cynical approach, they knew their constituents would not punish them for ignoring the wishes of the Alaskan people. However, by voting against Udall-Anderson, they could face a well-financed opponent in their next election.

John Dingell and Don Young reflected this strategy in their statements. It was John Dingell, the longest serving member of the House of Representatives and a true conservationist, who reminded his colleagues, "If a bill of the kind of the Udall-Anderson were to be before us dealing with Arizona, we would not be able to constrain the gentleman from Arizona; we would literally have to physically keep him in his seat because of the outrage he would feel about closing up massive areas of his state to business opportunity; massive areas of his state to mineral exploration; massive areas of his state to transportation, to hunting, and outdoor recreation, because that is what the proposal of the gentleman from Arizona does."

Just prior to voting, Don Young implored his colleagues to listen to the people of Alaska. He noted that, "Yes, the Governor, the two Senators, this Congressman, the legislature, and the majority of Alaskans feel that if the Udall-Anderson bill is adopted then the words of this Congress is no longer valid. Do you think this would happen in the states of California or New York? No, it would never happen. There would be a war tomorrow, a revolt on your hands. But we are far away, we are treated separately, treated differently and it is because we are not seen."

When it came time to vote, a tally of 268 to 157 adopted the Udall-Anderson Amendment. While both the Huckaby and Breaux Amendments were adopted by voice vote, they had no effect on what was sent to the U.S. Senate.

What was referred to the Senate Energy and Natural Resources Committee was a bill that protected more than 150 million acres of Alaska through various conservation classification systems. It was also much more restrictive in terms of limiting economic, recreational, and subsistence opportunities than either the Huckaby or Breaux proposals. One of the worst provisions was the creation of millions of acres of wilderness in the Chugach and Tongass National Forests. According to Don Young, "If the Udall-Anderson bill is adopted we are no doubt going to lose approximately 2,000 jobs. Regardless of what they say those are the figures that come down from the Administration."

If the Carter Administration or Chairman Udall thought the Senate would simply accept the House passed bill, they were badly mistaken. Unlike the House, the Senate has had a long-standing tradition of not passing legislation detrimental to the wishes of a particular state's elected officials. In this case, both Republican Senator Ted Stevens and Democrat Senator Mike Gravel were strongly opposed to the House passed version. Although Senator Gravel was not a member of the Senate Energy Committee, Senator Stevens was a member and he largely guided a compromise bill through the legislative process.

114

In the Senate Committee Report, Ted Stevens opined, "The Committee's product is extremely detailed and represents a balance of the issues with which it was confronted. While greatly different from the bill which I originally introduced in the 95th Congress, the Committee product is legislation which can be supported by Alaskans." The entire U.S. Senate approved the bill on August 19, 1980 by a vote of 78 to 14. The message loudly sent to the House was a "take it or leave it" approach.

For the next four months, the House opted to "leave it." This attitude changed dramatically on November 4, 1980. On that historic day, Ronald W. Reagan was elected the 40th President of the United States, Republicans seized control of the U.S. Senate for the first time since 1953, and the number of Republicans members in the House of Representatives increased from 158 to 191. What this meant was that Chairman Udall could accept the Senate passed bill or likely get nothing from the new Administration or Republican controlled Senate.

On November 12, 1980, the House of Representatives debated the Senate version of H.R. 39 in the lame duck session of the 96th Congress. Just eight days after President Carter was defeated, the House approved the Senate bill by voice vote. Prior to passage, Don Young remarked that, "I want to make it perfectly clear to my colleagues that I will not be voting for the passage of this legislation. I will tell you, though; it does contain many provisions that are good for Alaska. In this bill the good things are that in the Statehood Act lands are conveyed to the State. The existing Carter monuments are repealed. Access to inholdings and traditional access are guaranteed. There is maintenance in the timber industry in the Southeast and it is not being over-harvested. It is being harvested, as it should be. There are provisions for mineral development such as Borax in Chignik Creek, Greens Creek, et cetera. Most key mineral areas are open."

What President Carter signed into law on December 2, 1980 was the largest land bill in our nation's history. It affected some 157 million acres of Alaska. By comparison that is an area larger than the States of California, Maryland, Virginia and West Virginia combined. As a result of Public Law 96-487, 10 new and 3 existing parks were designated at 43 million acres. This unprecedented action doubled the size of the National Park System. Of the ten largest national parks, seven are now located in the State of Alaska. This includes the four largest of Wrangell-St Elias, Gates of the Arctic, Denali, and Katmai. By contrast, in 1994, the Congress established the fifth largest park, the Death Valley National Park, with a mere 3.3 million acres.

It also created 12 new national wildlife refuges and expanded four existing units. The total refuge acreage was 55 million. This doubled the size of the National Wildlife Refuge System and included the creation of the largest new refuge, the Arctic National Wildlife Refuge at 19.4 million acres. In fact, the ten biggest refuges within the National Wildlife Refuge System are all located in Alaska. They represent 76.7 million acres.

In addition, 25 Alaskan rivers were added to the Wild and Scenic River System; 14 wilderness areas totally 56.4 million acres were added to the federal land inventory; 2 National Monuments and 2 conservation areas were established; and 3.3 million acres were added to the National Forest System.

In terms of policy, a statutory preference was created for subsistence resource use within national parks and wildlife refuges; there was an expedited conveyance of federal lands to Alaskan natives; access for airplanes, motorboats, non-motorized vehicles, and snowmobiles was guaranteed; and all of Alaska's wildlife refuges are managed with an "Open until Closed" philosophy. According to the U.S. Fish and Wildlife Service's website, "All of the public lands in the (Alaska) refuges are open to both recreational and subsistence hunting and fishing."

All of these policy provisions were the result of the leadership of Don Young and Ted Stevens. The "Open until Closed" policy is exactly opposite from the rest of the 49 states. What this means is that the Fish and Wildlife Service can not routinely stop or curtail fishing, hunting, or trapping within any of Alaska's 16 refuge units.

Another key provision of the law was the requirement that the Secretary of Interior complete a two-year study on the 1.5 million acre Coastal Plain region of the Arctic National Wildlife Refuge (ANWR). This report offered the opportunity to judge whether oil and gas production should occur in this region and it provided an estimate of potential resources. Without Congressional approval, oil and gas development in ANWR is prohibited.

On April 20, 1987, then Secretary Don Hodel issued the required report which recommended that the Coastal Plain of ANWR be open to oil and gas leasing. Secretary Hodel noted, "Geologists consider the ANWR Coastal Plain the most outstanding onshore frontier area for prospective major oil discoveries in America. Estimates range between 600 million and 9.2 billion barrels of recoverable oil, the latter nearly equal to the Prudhoe Bay field.

Sadly, any real hope of Congress acting on the Secretary's favorable report was dashed on March 29, 1989, when the oil tanker *Exxon Valdez* struck Bligh Reef.

This environmental catastrophe caused the spilling of 10.8 million gallons of oil into the pristine Price William Sound killing fish, livelihoods, wildlife, and the opportunity to explore the ANWR Coastal Plain.

In the final analysis, the Alaska National Interest Lands Conservation Act of 1980 should not have become law. As Don Young asked during the debate on H.R. 39, "Do you think this would happen in the States of California or New York?" The answer was a resounding NO. In fact, such a massive designation of lands within a single state has never happened before or after H.R. 39.

As someone who diligently worked on this issue in 1980 for Congressman Richard T. Schulze (R-PA), I was deeply troubled that this legislation received final approval during a lame duck session of Congress. These sessions are normally reserved for "must pass" bills like increasing the federal debt limit or funding the operation of the U.S. government. Failure to pass them would result in a financial catastrophe. An Alaska lands bill was neither urgent nor necessary.

For Morris Udall, however, it was essential to move even a flawed bill because he understood this legislation would never pass during the Reagan Administration. For President Carter, who received the votes of 26 percent of Alaskans, he desperately wanted to sign

H.R. 39 into law to enhance his legacy. Sadly, the President did not seem to care that the Alaska National Interest Lands Conservation Act was highly unpopular in the 49th state.

Nevertheless, Don Young who represents all of Alaska noted, "The thing I object to most in this bill is it never should have been before us in the first place."

CHAPTER 5: HISTORIC ELECTION

On the morning of November 9, 1994, the American people woke up to hear that a massive earthquake had occurred during the night. While there were no injuries or deaths, the political landscape in Washington, D.C. had been literally turned upside down.

For the first time in 40 years, Republicans had gained control of the House of Representatives by picking up 54 seats. Among the casualties were the Speaker of the House, Thomas Foley (D-WA), the Chairman of the Ways and Means Committee, Dan Rostenkowski (D-IL), and the Chairman of the Judiciary Committee, Jack Brooks (D-TX). By losing his re-election to a 16th term to Republican George Nethercutt, Tom Foley became the 1st defeated Speaker since Galusha Grow of Scranton, Pennsylvania, who lost in 1862.

As someone who had worked on Capitol Hill for 17 years, I was tired of hearing Republicans called the loyal opposition or the permanent minority. Members of the Majority Party get to decide the legislative agenda. They control which bills will get a hearing, a mark-up, and movement in the House of Representatives. As a member of the minority party, you have little input into the legislative process, your views are frequently ignored, and your vote is seldom solicited. Who controls the People's House is of enormous importance and after 40 years in the political wilderness, the Election of 1994 was epic. There was an expectation Republicans would gain seats in President William Clinton's first midterm, however, no political pundits predicted the shocking magnitude of this election.

When I woke up on that Wednesday morning, I had bittersweet emotions. I was thrilled that the Republicans had finally gained control of the People's House. I was also apprehensive because the House Merchant Marine and Fisheries Committee, which I had served on for ten years, was likely to be abolished. In fact, it was on December 7, 1994, the 53rd anniversary of the Pearl Harbor attack.

As the Republican Chief-of-Staff of the Merchant Marine and Fisheries Committee, I was afforded the opportunity to meet with the Chairman of the Republican Conference Committee, future Speaker John Boehner. He assured me there were thousands of jobs available for the Republican staff that lost theirs on November 8, 1995. It was his job to serve as a clearinghouse for all the new administrative and legislative Committee staff that would be required to operate the House of Representatives. Twenty-two years later, I am still waiting for that call.

Fortunately, the new Chairman of the newly renamed Committee on Resources, Don Young was willing to provide employment for me and my colleagues Bonnie Bruce, Linda Livingston, Elizabeth Megginson, Kathleen Miller, Lisa Pittman, John Clark Rayfield, Lisa Rulli, Ann Vogt, David Whaley and Margherita Woods. On Election Day, he had been re-elected to an 11th full term with 58 percent of the vote to represent all Alaskans.

Several days after the election, I was visited by then Chairman of the Merchant Marine and Fisheries Committee, Gerry Studds. During his chairmanship, I had worked closely with his staff including his outstanding Chief-of-Staff Jeff Pike. They were always gracious and interested in my point of view. In fact, I was invited to their monthly scheduling meeting where decisions were made as to which bills would be heard and marked up in the future. This courtesy was rare on Capital Hill.

Without a hint of a smile, Gerry Studds told me he was thinking about asking for a recount in his November 8th re-election, which he won by 94,000 votes. I was stunned by this statement but not surprised because on that fateful day he lost both his Chairmanship and his beloved Committee. I was also a little sad because Gerry Studds was a superb legislator, effective representative for his District, and a caring human being.

The Committee on Resources can trace its storied history back more than 200 years. After the Louisiana Purchase in

123

1803, it was unclear as to which House Committee would manage the newly acquired 53 million acres. These lands more than doubled the size of the United States. On December 17, 1805, the Committee on Public Lands was established with jurisdiction over the lands of the United States. The first Chairman of the Committee was Andrew Gregg of Carlisle, Pennsylvania and one of its most famous members was John F. Lacey of Iowa. Chairman Lacey was the author of the so-called Lacey Act of 1900 and the Antiquities Act of 1906. Five future U.S. Presidents including John Quincy Adams, William Henry Harrison, Andrew Johnson, Rutherford B. Hayes, and John A. Garfield had served on the Public Lands Committee.

On January 3, 1995, Don Young was one of 230 Republicans who took the oath of office. The new Minority Leader Richard Gephardt (D-MO) said, "With resignation but with resolve, I hereby end 40 years of Democratic rule of the House." In response, new Speaker Newt Gingrich (R-GA) opined, "Here we are as commoners together, to some extent Democrats and Republicans, to some extent liberals and conservatives, but Americans all." In its January 5, 1995 edition, the voice of Capitol Hill, *Roll Call,* had as its newspaper headline, "Republicans Sworn In to 104th as Hill's New 'Power Rangers.'"

For Don Young it was the end of 22 long years of serving in the minority. On

January 3rd, he became the 65th Chairman of the House Resources Committee. He is the only representative from Alaska who has ever been elected to this position. As Chairman he was responsible for choosing the five Republican Subcommittee Chairmen; appointing all Republican staff; preparing and defending the Committee's Annual Budget; writing the Committee's Oversight Plan that was submitted to House leadership; reviewing all proposed public hearings; and approving all Committee travel.

Unlike other previous Congresses, Don Young, like the rest of his Republican colleagues, was limited to six years of service as Chairman. This was an effort to allow younger Republican Members of Congress greater input into the legislative process. In addition, the Republican Conference voted to eliminate earmarks, which gave members an opportunity to specifically designate in legislation an airport, bridge, or flood control project in their district.

In both cases, these changes were a terrible mistake. By limiting members to an arbitrary term limit, what has happened is that many members simply retired after their six years and took with them invaluable experiences. By outlawing earmarks, control over taxpayer money was ceded to unelected bureaucrats and it made the legislative process much more difficult by denying Chairmen the ability to obtain a buy-in from their colleagues. A member is much more likely to support an aviation, highway, or water resources bill, if there is a project within their district.

The Young Family

Don, Lu, Dawn and Jodi

Don Young, Speaker of the House Carl
Albert and Republican Leader Gerald Ford

Congressman Don Young

President Nixon Signing into Law Authorization for the Trans-Alaska Pipeline
November 16, 1973

L-R Sen. Mike Gravel, Sen. Henry Jackson, Sec. Interior Rog Morton, Sen. Ted Stevens, Cong. James Haley
Cong. John Melcher, Cong. Harold Johnson, Sen. Paul Fannin, Cong. Don Young, Cong. Craig Hosmer

131

President Gerald Ford signing Fishery
Conservation and Management Act of
1976

President Jimmy Carter signing Alaska
National Interest Lands Conservation Act

President Ronald Reagan, Congressman
John Miller and Congressman Don Young
at the signing of the Fishing Vessel Safety
Act

President Ronald Reagan and
Congressman Don Young

President George H.W. Bush and
Congressman Don Young

President Bill Clinton and Congressman
Don Young at the signing of a bill
beneficial to Alaska natives.

President George W. Bush and
Congressman Don Young at
SAFETEA-LU Bill Signing

Congressman Don Young, Senator Ted
Stevens and Senator Frank Murkowski

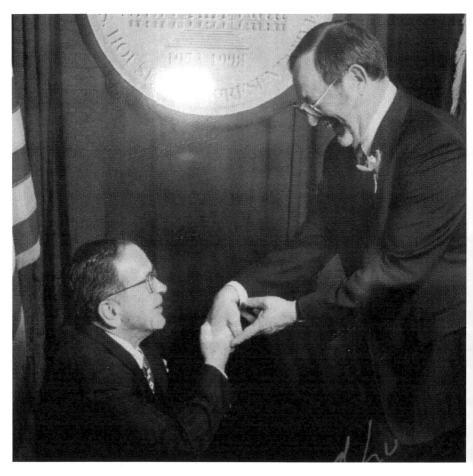

Senator Ted Stevens and Congressman
Don Young

Speaker of the House John Boehner and
Congressman Don Young

Senator Lisa Murkowski, Congressman
Don Young and Senator Dan Sullivan

Congressman Don Young campaigning in
Anchorage, Alaska

Harry Burroughs and Congressman Don
Young

Congressman Don Young, Senator Lisa
Murkowski and Senator Dan Sullivan
celebrate allowing energy exploration
within the 1002 Area of the Arctic National
Wildlife Refuge

Congressman Don Young, Anne Young,
Speaker of the House Paul Ryan and
Congressman Young's Washington staff

Congressman Don Young on the
steps of the U.S. Capitol

Anne Walton Young and Don Young on
their Wedding Day at the U.S. Capitol

CHAPTER 6: CHAIRMAN OF RESOURCES COMMITTEE

On January 11, 1995, the Resources Committee met for an organizational meeting of the 104th Congress. As directed by Chairman Young, each Republican staffer was wearing a name badge, which designated whether they worked for the Full Committee or one of its five Subcommittees. While I thought this was an excellent way for new members and new staff to recognize each other, it did conjure up images of one of my favorite movies, *The Treasure of the Sierra Madre.* In that Academy Award winning 1948 picture, Humphrey Bogart asks a Mexican bandit, "If you're the police, where are your badges?" He replies, "Badges ... we ain't got no badges. We don't need no badges. I don't have to show you any stinking badges." For the record, I have proudly kept my badges.

For the next six years, the Resources Committee set a remarkable record of legislative achievement. Don Young allowed his Subcommittee Chairmen flexibility to conduct hearings and mark-ups of their choosing, he was willing to move bills drafted by Democrats, and he respected the rights of his colleagues to represent their constituents. Unlike Morris Udall, he never dictated that a national forest, national park, national wildlife refuge, or wilderness area would be established or expanded over the objections of the member who represented that District or State. In fact, he was willing to move bills that expanded the federal land inventory despite his own objections. If a member wanted a national park in their district, he was willing to move their bill through the legislative process.

As the Staff Director of the Subcommittee on Fisheries, Wildlife, and Oceans, we had jurisdiction over legislation that was previously referred to the House Merchant Marine and Fisheries Committee. We had an outstanding and effective Subcommittee Chairman, Jim Saxton of Mount Holly, New Jersey. Jim Saxton was a skilled legislator and a tremendous advocate for the citizens of New Jersey's Third Congressional District, which reelected him to 12 consecutive terms. Upon his retirement announcement in December 2007, Don Young told his colleagues that Jim Saxton, "was a superb Subcommittee Chairman who sponsored a number of important conservation measures that became law. His constituents living in Cherry Hill, Mount Holly, and Toms River, New Jersey will miss Jim Saxton and his lifelong advocacy of Theodore Roosevelt's vision and principles. I wish him calm sailing days beyond Congress. 'May the wind always be on your back and the sunshine upon your face.'"

I was also blessed to have a dedicated, professional, and talented Subcommittee staff. We would not have been successful without the efforts of

Bonnie Bruce, Dawn Criste, Robert Howarth, Joseph Love, Sharon McKenna, Kathleen Miller, John Clark Rayfield, Jeff Ripp, Lisa Rulli, Michelle Sparck, and David Whaley.

During his six years as Chairman of the Resources Committee, Don Young had an impressive record of achievement because of his hard work, leadership, and vision. Between 1995 and 2000, the Full Committee, its Subcommittees, and Special Task Forces, held 558 legislative and oversight hearings. These included hearings on the Arctic National Wildlife Refuge, Endangered Species Act, Marine Mammal Protection Act, National Wildlife Refuge System, Outer Continental Shelf Production, Stellar Sea Lions, Tongass National Forest, and Trans-Alaskan Pipeline.

Thousands of public and private witnesses were given the chance to articulate their views on hundreds of pieces of legislation. As a result of the Committee's work, a number of important bills were signed into law by President William J. Clinton. Among the most memorable were: Bikini Resettlement and Relocation Act (P.L. 106-100); Designation of Martin Luther King's Memorial in our Nation's Capitol (P.L. 105-201); Migratory Bird Treaty Reform Act (P.L. 105-312); National Wildlife Refuge System Improvement Act (P.L. 105-57); Omnibus Parks and Public Lands Management Act (P.L. 104-333); Quincy Library Group

Forest Recovery Act (P.L. 105-277); and
Sustainable Fisheries Act (P.L. 104-297).

When the final tally was made more
than 600 Resources bills passed both
bodies of Congress resulting in 508 public
laws. While Republicans controlled the
House and the Senate during Don Young's
Chairmanship, William J. Clinton, a
Democrat, was the President of the United
States. It was, therefore, necessary to work
in a collaborative fashion with the Clinton
Administration. These efforts were
successful because Don Young was a
master of the legislative process. He was
willing to fight hard for his beliefs, while
embracing the philosophy of William
Shakespeare that, "Perfect is the Enemy of
the Good."

In the 106th Congress, 202 Resource
generated bills were enacted into law. This
was 33 percent of the total of 613 public
laws approved by the entire Congress in
1999 and 2000. Over the six years of his
Chairmanship, Don Young had 31
Resource bills that he sponsored which
were signed into law. Of that total, 13 were
specific to the State of Alaska including
efforts to amend the Alaska Native Claims
Settlement Act, Glacier Bay National Park
Boundary Adjustment Act, Green Creek
Land Exchange Act, Hood Bay Land
Exchange Act, Indian Health Care
Improvement Act, Mollie Beattie Alaska
Wilderness Act, Pribilof Islands Transition
Act, and Yukon River Salmon Act. This is a
remarkable record and I am going to

highlight three landmark statutes that originated in my Subcommittee on Fisheries, Wildlife, and Oceans.

The first measure was the Sustainable Fisheries Act of 1996. This legislation was a reauthorization of the Fishery Conservation and Management Act of 1976. Although the original law had stopped the destruction of our fishery stocks by foreign vessels, there were additional modifications that required further legislative action.

On January 4, 1995, Don Young introduced his first bill of the 104th Congress, H.R. 39, the Fishery Conservation and Management Amendments. This legislation established new national standards to prevent overfishing, rebuild fish stocks, minimize the mortality of fish bycatch, and promote the safety of human life at sea. These standards are used by the eight Regional Fishery Management Councils to write new or updated management plants for a variety of fisheries species.

The bill changed the structure of the Councils, required rebuilding overfished stocks, mandated the identification of essential fish habitat, and stipulated that the North Pacific Fishery Management Council was authorized to use incentives and fines to achieve bycatch reductions. Bycatch is a serious problem in many American fisheries. When catching herring, mackerel, salmon, and tuna, it is not unusual to land millions of pounds of non-targeted fish species. These are called bycatch.

As the Captain of a fishing vessel, you are required to obtain a permit to fish for a specific species. There may be a market for the bycatch but they are prohibited from selling it. Ship captains are also not interested in storing fish that have no financial value. In most cases, their only real option is to dump these fish - living and dead - back into the ocean. While there are observes on most U.S. fishing ships, it is difficult to calculate the exact number and financial value of bycatch species.

In December 2013, the National Marine Fisheries Service (NMFS) issued its first assessment of the problem in its *U.S. National Bycatch Report*. In its analysis, NMFS, "Estimated 2010 fish bycatch for the U.S. commercial fisheries totaled a little more than 607 million pounds and about 5.8 million individual fish." Sadly, the problem still exists and there is no denying that bycatch is a terrible waste of a valuable resource. These fish could provide badly needed protein to millions of homeless, poor, and starving Americans.

On May 10, 1995, the Resources Committee met to mark-up H.R. 39. There were 18 Democrat and Republican amendments offered and 17 were adopted. The legislation was favorably reported to the House of Representatives by voice vote. In the Committee report on H.R. 39, we learned that, "The Committee identified several key areas of concern to be addressed in this legislation." These included, "Bycatch reduction, habitat protection, identification and protecting of stocks nearing an overfished condition, rebuilding of overfished stocks, reform of Fishery Management Councils, establishment of the Bering Sea Community Development Quota Program, and a program for fishing capacity reduction." This last provision was designed to solve the problem of too many ships chasing too few fish.

The Fishery Conservation and Management Act Amendments were considered in the House on October 18, 1995. During general debate, Don Young noted, "This legislation enjoys broad, bipartisan support from members of the Resources Committee and those members from coastal districts with fishing interests. It is full of compromise. Yet does not compromise on maintaining the health of the resource which should be the goal of everyone here."

Ranking Subcommittee Member Gerry Studds said, "The bill represents something that is so rare in these chambers of late - a bipartisan effort to protect our natural resources, and in turn benefit our economy. I urge members to support this bill and oppose any efforts to weaken it." In the spirit of bipartisanship, 12 amendments were offered to improve H.R. 39. These amendments addressed country of Origin Designation, Individual Transferrable Quotas, Pacific Insular Territories, and "Optimum Yield Definition. " All of these modifications were adopted and the legislation was approved on a 388 to 37 vote. This was a remarkable achievement and a tribute to Don Young on his willingness to work with his colleagues on this vital piece of legislation.

After the Senate version, S.39 was adopted on September 19, 1996 on a 100 to 0 vote; the House gave its final approval to this legislation on September 27, 1996. Prior to voting, Don Young was honest in his assessment of S. 39, "In my opinion the House passed bill is a much stronger bill. However, in the waning days of this Congress, we are in a position of accepting a weaker bill or accomplish nothing for fisheries conservation and management. I urge all members to support passage of S. 39 and send this important piece of fishery management and conservation to the President."

Later in the debate, Gerry Studds opined, "I rise with mixed emotions to support the passage of this bill. The Magnuson Act was the first substantive piece of legislation I coauthored when I came to Congress in 1973, the same year the gentleman from Alaska came. So it is somewhat fitting that it will also be one of the last bills in my career here."

In his October 11, 1996 signing statement on the Sustainable Fisheries Act, President William J. Clinton echoed a familiar theme that, "This Act represents a bipartisan effort to address the problems facing our nation's fisheries, both commercial and recreational, and will greatly improve the future management of important fishery resources."

At the end of the 104th Congress, Gerry Studds retired from Congress. His leaving was a tremendous loss for the residents of Massachusetts 10th District and coastal fishing communities throughout the United States. It was also a loss for Don Young who told his House colleagues that, "I have great respect for the gentleman from Massachusetts and his efforts in the fisheries field. I do thank him for his love for the sea and the fishermen he has served. I will cherish the advice that the gentleman from Massachusetts can give me on this issue as he goes into another life."

In 2006, the Congress reauthorized this vital fisheries statute by passing the Magnuson-Stevens Fishery Conservation and Management Reauthorization Act. Don Young was the leading advocate for this important legislation. One of the provisions of P.L. 109-479 was to rename the statute the Magnuson-Stevens Fishery Conservation and Management Act. How ironic that the two U.S. Senators are recognized but not the original two House sponsored, Gerry Studds and Don Young.

Sadly, this is how the legislative process often works. The U.S. Senate is filled with "show horses" that work overtime to book television interviews and claim credit for nearly every legislative achievement. I will never forget how Texas Senator Phil Gramm opposed funding for a new veterans hospital in Houston, but when it was time to cut the ribbon, he was holding the scissors.

In most cases, the hard work and heavy lifting of moving a bill with hearings and mark-ups occurs in the People's House. These are the real "work horses." I, therefore, look forward to the day when this law accurately reflects its parenthood by being called the Magnuson, Stevens, Studds, and Young Fishery Conservation and Management Act.

It is also indisputable that this law has had a tremendous economic impact on the State of Alaska. In 2014, the Alaskan Seafood Industry employed 41,200 people. This represented about 20 percent of Alaska's basic private sector economy. It contributed to federal, local, and state authorities nearly $140 million in fees, self-assessments, and taxes. It provided $5.8 billion in annual labor income and $14.6 billion in economic output.

Salmon is still king in Alaska. This fishery contributed 38,400 full-time-equivalent jobs and $2 billion in annual labor income to the national economy. Alaska led the nation with landings of 5.98 million pounds. The three major landing ports are Dutch Harbor, Kodiak, and the Aleutian Islands. These American fisheries will continue to provide millions of pounds of healthy, nutritional, and sustainable cod, crab, Pollock, and salmon to consumers in the future. None of this would have been achievable in Alaska without the leadership of Don Young.

In 1992, the U.S. Fish and Wildlife Service was sued by the Defenders of Wildlife, the National Audubon Society, and the Wilderness Society for allowing activities which they believed harmed fish, habitat, and wildlife. Instead of going to court, the agency settled the suit in October 1993 by agreeing to terminate specific activities that they determined were not compatible with refuge purposes. These included farming, grazing, and motorized recreation. Under the leadership of Director Mollie Beattie, refuge managers were given broad discretion to determine what activities were compatible and to prohibit certain wildlife dependent recreational activities - like hunting and fishing - when sufficient funds were not available to manage those uses. The agency used the Refuge Recreation Act of 1962 to justify denying access to thousands of Americans.

As you might expect, there was a huge uproar from the fishing, hunting, and conservation community. Members of these groups were incensed that they were being denied access to federal lands, which they had paid for with excise taxes, and federal duck stamp purchases. It was, therefore, not surprising that one of the first conversations I had with new Chairman Don Young was with regard to his directive that the refuge access problem would be solved. As a result, an organic act, which establishes the rules of governing, for the National Wildlife Refuge System was one of his highest legislative priorities in the 104th Congress.

On May 18, 1995, Don Young, John Dingell, Bill Brewster, Billy Tauzin, and Jim Saxton, introduced the National Wildlife Refuge System Improvement Act. In his floor statement, Don Young said, "This legislation would be the first comprehensive refuge reform bill since the enactment of the National Wildlife Refuge System Administration Act of 1966. While it is appropriate to periodically review the compatibility of certain activities, there is no statutory list of purposes for the National Wildlife Refuge System and no statutory definition of what constitutes a compatible use of a refuge. Without this guidance, individual wildlife managers have broad discretion to prevent or disallow recreational activities which do not materially affect the purposes of the refuge or the refuge system."

A key component of H.R. 1675 was contained within Section 3 dealing with the mission and purposes of the system. Specifically, the language said, "To provide opportunities for compatible fish and wildlife dependent recreation, including fishing and hunting, wildlife observation, and environmental education."

While the Clinton Administration initially supported the legislation, this changed on December 15, 1995 when Secretary of the Interior Bruce Babbitt issued a Press Release stating, "He could no longer support H.R. 1675, because of crippling amendments and new interpretations of key provisions in the Committee report."

On April 24, 1996, H.R. 1675 was considered in the House. It was supported by the American Archery Council, the American Sportfishing Association, B.A.S.S., California Waterfowl Association, Congressional Sportsmen's Foundation, Foundation for North American Wild Sheep, International Association of Fish and Wildlife Agencies, International Bowhunters Association, Masters of Foxhounds Association of America, National Rifle Association, National Wild Turkey Federation, North American Waterfowl Federation, Quail Unlimited, Ruffed Grouse Society, Safari Club International, Wildlife Forever, and the Wildlife Legislative Fund of America.

As the floor manager of the legislation, Don Young remarked,

"Regrettably, in recent years the public's confidence in our refuge system has been shaken by arbitrary decisions made by refuge mangers; the diversion of funds to other higher profile issues; the elimination of all existing uses on newly acquired refuge lands; lawsuits designed to prohibit certain secondary uses on a refuge; and the lack of either a vision or a comprehensive plan on how our refuge system will be managed in the future."

Despite the objections of the Clinton Administration, the House approved H.R. 1675 by a vote of 287 to 138. Sadly, there was no action on the issue by either the Senate Environment and Public Works Committee or the entire U.S. Senate. While H.R. 1675 could have been held "at the desk," the Republican Senate leadership opted not to take that approach. .

On February 4, 1997, Don Young, John Dingell, John Tanner, and Randy "Duke" Cunningham re-introduced the National Wildlife Refuge System Improvement Act of 1997. In his opening statement on H.R. 511 at the Subcommittee on Fisheries Conservation, Wildlife, and Oceans hearing, Don Young noted that, "I remain hopeful that Secretary Babbitt will soon respond to the offer John Dingell and I made to him on December 5, 1996, to discuss those provisions in H.R. 511 that may continue to cause concern within the Administration." Don Young was interested in winning the war and not just a simple battle.

In a rare appearance before a Subcommittee, Secretary Bruce Babbitt testified on H.R. 511 and H.R. 512, a bill that would require a Congressional authorization of any new wildlife refuge. Bruce Babbitt said, "I would like to state at the outset in a spirit of frankness and candor that I am strongly opposed to both of these bills, and I would be compelled to recommend that the President veto either one or both if they are enacted in their present form." However, this was not the last word. During the question and answer period, in response to an inquiry from Richard Pombo of California, Bruce Babbitt responded that, "When I spoke with Congressman Dingell yesterday, he said to me can we find common ground. And what I said to him, I say to you, Mr. Congressman, I believe that we ought to try."

Upon leaving the hearing, Chairman Young and Secretary Babbitt had a brief conversation outside of 1327 Longworth House Office Building. They mutually agreed to try to work out their differences. As a result, negotiations convened in Secretary Babbitt's Conference Room at the Main Interior Building. We met for six consecutive Friday mornings. Those negotiating were me on behalf of Don Young; Dan Beattie for John Dingell; Chris Mann for George Miller; Don Berry for the Department of Interior; Dan Ashe for the U.S. Fish and Wildlife Service; William P. Horn for the

Wildlife Legislative Fund of America; Max Peterson and Gary Taylor for the International Association of Fish and Wildlife Agencies; Daniel Beard for the National Audubon Society; and Rollie Sparrowe for the Wildlife Management Institute.

As the moderator of the group, Bruce Babbitt was a gracious and honest broker. While the discussions were difficult, each negotiator was given an opportunity to articulate what they needed in the legislation, to list any shortcomings or problem areas, to identify their "bottom line," and to confirm their willingness to seek a compromise.

The result of these talks were incorporated within a new bill, H.R. 1420, the National Wildlife Refuge System Improvement Act of 1997. The fundamental provisions were: it established a system-wide "conservation mission" for our nation's national wildlife refuge units; it defined "wildlife-dependent recreation" to mean hunting, fishing, wildlife observation and photography, or environmental education; it established a process for determining a "compatible use;" it required the U.S. Fish and Wildlife Service to make an interim determination on whether wildlife dependent uses could continue during the implementation of a management plan; it established as U.S. policy that wildlife-dependent recreational uses are legitimate, appropriate uses, and shall be facilitated throughout the refuge system; and it required the completion of a comprehensive conservation plan for each refuge.

On April 30, 1997, the Natural Resources Committee considered H.R. 1420. There were no amendments offered and the Committee ordered the bill reported to the House of Representatives. I suspect the lack of any proposed modifications was Bruce Babbitt's letter to Chairman Young a day earlier. In that correspondence, the Secretary stated, "As we discussed, our agreement is to seek passage of the bill as introduced, and any substantive change would obligate the parties now supporting it to re-evaluate their positions."

On June 3, 1997, H.R. 1420 was considered in the House. As the chief sponsor, Don Young told his colleagues, "H.R. 1420 is the product of many long hours of thoughtful negotiations between the Department of the Interior, the original sponsor of the bill, the staff of Congressman George Miller, and those representing the hunting, conservation, and environmental communities. In particular, I want to compliment Secretary Bruce Babbitt for his personal commitment to this effort and for hosting these discussions. This process could well serve as a model to resolve other legislative differences. This is a sound piece of conservation legislation that is true to the legacy of Theodore Roosevelt."

During the debate on H.R. 1420, several House members expressed their support for the legislation. John Dingell said, "I do want to say one word about the gentleman from Alaska, my good friend. I know he had strong differences with the Secretary early on, and I know the Secretary had strong differences with my colleague. The two came together in a fashion which does credit not only to them but to this institution and to their respective responsibilities."

The ranking Democrat member of the Resources Committee, George Miller, who opposed H.R. 511, stated, "I would like to commend Secretary Babbitt for taking the time and the initiative to bring disparate sides together to negotiate. I would also like to commend Messrs. Dingell and Young for their willingness to seek common ground. They never wavered in their support for the refuge system."

When the roll was called, I was stunned to see that H.R. 1420 passed by a vote of 407 to 1. It is rare that such a complex and important bill passes with virtually no opposition. It was a tribute to Don Young on his willingness to work in a bipartisan manner to improve our nation's wildlife refuge system for all Americans.

The lone dissent was the NO vote of Ron Paul of Texas. While he choose not to speak on the bill, he did submit a statement for the Congressional Record that says in part, "In an attempt to assist in the fulfillment of important international treaty obligations of the United States, today we are asked to support a bill which reinforces an unconstitutional program of the Johnson Administration, the National Wildlife Refuge Act of 1966."

While this was a tremendous victory, this was only half the battle to enact this legislation into law. The U.S. Senate has a well-deserved reputation of being a body where good bills go to die. On more than one occasion, I lamented that we have a bicameral and not a unicameral national legislature. It is difficult to pass anything in the U.S. Senate because of the need for 60 votes, and Senators are constantly on the prowl for vehicles to carry their favorite legislative ideas.

In an effort to avoid this problem, Don Young reached out to Senate Majority Leader Trent Lott (R-MS) to urge him to hold H.R. 1420 "at the desk." What this meant was the bill would not be referred to a Senate Committee including the Environment and Public Works Committee. According to an internal memo written by Senate leadership staff to Trent Lott a decision to hold the bill at the desk, "Distressed Senator Kempthorne who wants to get the bill referred so he can add his Endangered Species Act reforms (which I believe are flawed at best – despite his assertions to the contrary)." If

H.R. 1420 had not been held at the desk, it is likely that it would not have been enacted into law. Amendments to the Endangered Species Act are highly controversial and it would be nearly impossible to obtain 60 votes in the U.S. Senate.

In their letter to Senator Lott on June 9, 1997, Don Young and Jim Saxton wrote, "It is more important than ever that the Congress approve H.R. 1420 as it is currently written. If it is not, we risk losing a significant conservation initiative that will benefit the 92-million acre National Wildlife Refuge System well into the next century."

Even before any action by the upper body, Secretary Bruce Babbitt was thinking ahead. In a memorandum for the President, Babbitt wrote, "I am bringing this to your attention because this legislation (H.R. 1420) is a real legacy achievement. When the bill comes up, you ought to consider a signing ceremony somewhere down south where this will be a big issue for sportsmen, especially duck hunters. Arkansas in autumn comes to mind."

On September 10, 1997, the U.S. Senate approved H.R. 1420 with three minor changes by unanimous consent. Two weeks later, the House concurred with the amendments. In his floor statement, Don Young said, "The three differences in the legislation include: an

168

expanded definition of the term "compatible use," a requirement that the Secretary monitor the status and trends of fish, wildlife, and plants in each refuge, and a clarification regarding existing rights-of-way within refuges. I have carefully reviewed these changes and find them acceptable." This time the final vote was 419 to 1 with Ron Paul again casting the dissenting vote.

Instead of choosing Arkansas, President William J. Clinton signed H.R. 1420 in the Oval Office of the White House. Don Young was present for the signing and he got to hear the President say, "The bill is proof that when there is a shared commitment to do what is right for our natural resources, partisan and ideological differences can be set aside and compromises can be negotiated for the benefit of the common good."

After 30 years of unsuccessfully trying to write a comprehensive organic law for the National Wildlife Refuge System, Don Young was able to build a unique coalition of environmental, hunting, and wildlife conservation organizations. The value of a law is best assessed over time. It is now 20 years since the enactment of P.L. 105-57. The National Wildlife Refuge System Improvement Act of 1997 has been a tremendous success. It has never been amended. It will stand the test of time as one of the most important conservation laws in the last 100 years.

On October 13, 1995, one of the most infamous dove hunts in U.S. history occurred in Dixie County, Florida. Florida State Senator Charles Williams who had aspirations about running for the U.S. Congress hosted it. It was a charity hunt to raise funds for the Florida Sheriffs Youth ranches, a non-profit organization, that operates ranch facilities for abused, at risk, or orphan children in the state. Many of these children were involved in juvenile delinquency, petty crimes, and some suffered serious emotional problems.

By way of background, the United States and Great Britain signed a Convention for the Protection of Migratory Birds in 1916. Two years later, the U.S. Congress passed the implementing law, the Migratory Bird Treaty Act (MBTA). In 1935, the Secretary of Interior issued regulations for migratory bird hunting including the practice of "baiting" which is the placement of corn, wheat, or other grain to attract or lure birds to a specific location for hunting.

The Second Annual Dove Hunt was held on the 600-acre farm owned by Herman Sanchez of Cross City, Florida. At 1:00 p.m. the hunt commenced and about 250 participants were assigned a specific area to shoot doves. After about three hours, 10 law enforcement agents of the U.S. Fish and Wildlife Service abruptly stopped the event. The agent in charge told Senator Williams, who was not hunting, that the agency had received a tip the night before the hunt that a portion of the Sanchez property had been baited with corn to attract doves.

The agents then proceeded to issue citations to 88 individuals for violating the MBTA. Those arrested included three county Sheriffs, city and county commissioners, clerks of the court, local mayors, Florida prison officials, and a Regional Director of the Florida Game and Freshwater Commission. They were charged with breaking Section 20.21 (i) that says, "No person shall take migratory birds by the aid of baiting, or over any baited area." Their crime was a Class B misdemeanor. Those citied had two options: pay the fines of $250 plus $25 for each bird taken or seek a hearing before an Administrative law judge. Most hunters paid the fines that amounted to $39,000 for 488 dead doves.

The Administrative law judge option was rejected because it was expensive, time consuming, and likely to fail. This is because in 1995 most federal courts were using a strict liability legal doctrine for migratory bird baiting cases. What this meant was if you were on the Sanchez farm, you had a gun in your hard, and had harvested doves then you were guilty. Those charged did not get their day in court, the federal government did not need to prove intent, and the location of the "bait" was irrelevant. In fact, several hunters were convicted despite the fact that the "bait" was more than a mile from where they hunted. There was no legal defense in these cases.

A good example of the type of people who participated in the charity hunt was Sheriff Larry Edmonds of Dixie County, Florida. Sheriff Edmonds told the local media that, "The irony of the whole thing is that I didn't like to dove hunt, and I was only on the field that day because I felt an obligation to be there to support the Youth Ranches. I don't intend to shoot anymore doves because it's too hard to do it legally when they have laws like this and this is a bad law."

A second participant was Bill Boe, a twice-wounded Vietnam veteran who stated, "We were invited guests at the hunt and we went there in support of the youth ranches on invitation from Senator Williams." He went on to tell the media that the raid "was intended to be a big bust, so that important people in the community and throughout the state would look bad." On that count, they were successful. State Senator Williams decided not to run for Congress because of the embarrassment and the negative press he received in this case.

As Chairman of the Resources Committee with jurisdiction of the Migratory Bird Treaty Act, Don Young believed that the use of the strict liability doctrine was fundamentally wrong. The U.S. Fish and Wildlife Service should have stopped the Dixie County hunt before it even started. Their job is to protect wildlife resources and not simply watch the fine meter increase with each dying dove.

Ironically, Congress had never passed a law that says: this is baiting and this practice is illegal. In fact, it was not illegal to bait a field or to feed migratory birds. It was, however, strictly prohibited to hunt in such an area. On May 15, 1997, the Subcommittee on Fisheries Conservation, Wildlife, and Oceans conducted a hearing on the application of strict liability. William P. Horn, former Assistant Secretary of the Interior testified, "The imposition of strict liability eliminates the ability of a hunter or landowner to mount a defense against charges of illegal baiting. And this is completely contrary to the fundamental premise of American justice that one is innocent until proven guilty."

A second witness was Bill Boe who testified on behalf of the Alpha Gamma Rho agricultural fraternity at the University of Florida. In his statement, he said, "When my license was taken that day I was indicted, tried, and convicted in the field. The next letter I got was a letter stating you have the option of mailing in your money or perhaps --- you can use Visa or MasterCard. If you go to court and are found guilty, you will pay up to $500 and possibly spend one year in federal prison."

As a result of the hearing, Don Young introduced with John Dingell, John Tanner (D-TN), and Cliff Sterns (R-FL), H.R. 2863, the Migratory Bird Treaty Reform Act. In his introductory statement, Don Young said, "The fundamental purpose of this legislation is to provide clear guidance to hunters, landowners, law enforcement officials, wildlife managers, and courts on what the restrictions are on the taking of migratory birds. This will not weaken the restrictions on the method and manner of taking migratory birds, nor will it weaken the protection of the resource. It will, however, allow individuals to have their day in court."

On April 29, 1998, the Full Resources Committee met to consider H.R. 2883. Don Young offered an amendment that limited the scope of the bill to the replacement of "strict liability" with the "knew or should have known" standard. The amendment and the bill were reported to the House of Representatives by voice vote.

In 1978, the Fifth Circuit Court ruled in the United States v Delahoussaye case that the prosecution must show that the person "should have known" that the area was baited. By so doing, the 5th Circuit, which hears cases from Louisiana, Mississippi, and Texas, became the first federal court to break with the strict liability interpretation. According to the Senate Environment and Public Works Committee, "The record indicates that this legal standard (should have known) has, in no matter, lessened the conviction of persons who, by the evidence presented, have violated the baiting prohibitions."

There is a reason why strict liability is not used in most criminal cases. For instance, can you imagine if a policeman could pull your car over and cite you for driving under the influence because the policeman observed you leaving a bar. This is strict liability. Fortunately, the policeman must prove that your blood alcohol exceeded the state's mandated level.

On September 10, 1998, the House considered H.R. 2863. As the author, Don Young accurately described the problem, "Under strict liability, if you are hunting in a field that an agent determines is baited, whether you knew it or not, you are guilty. There is no defense and any evidence you may have to support your position is irreverent. It does not matter whether there was a ton of grain or three kernels, whether this feed served as an attraction to migratory birds, or even how far the "bait" is from the hunting site. If you believe that every American is innocent until proven guilty and that a person should be entitled to offer evidence in their defense, then you should vote for this legislation."

The opponents of this legislation used the argument of the U.S. Fish and Wildlife Service that baiting convictions would be difficult if the Congress eliminated the strict liability standard. In our free society, ease of enforcement should not be the standard when applying the law. If their law enforcement job is more difficult, then so be it.

This was also a fallacious argument. Between 1984 and 1997, the U.S. Fish and Wildlife Service issued 2,318 citations in the three southern states that use the "knew or should have known" legal standard. The agency obtained a guilty ruling in 2,042 cases, which was a conviction rate of 88 percent. There were no migratory bird populations put at risk and the Service never tried to overturn or challenge the Delahoussaye decision.

Don Young also submitted for the Record a letter signed by Larry D. Closson, the Chief Law Enforcement Officer for the Illinois Department of Natural Resources. Larry Closson wrote, "As a career conservation law enforcement officer, I know first hand the strengths and weaknesses of our current federal baiting regulations. If Congress adopts the Delahoussaye standard for waterfowl baiting, a serious and longstanding weakness will have been remedied."

At the completion of debate, 322 members voted for H.R. 2863 and 90 cast a negative vote. A majority of Democrats, including Minority Whip Steny Hoyer of Maryland, voted for the measure and only three Republicans were opposed. Even Ron Paul of Texas voted for the bill.

On October 5, 1998, the Senate Environment and Public Works Committee reported an amended version of H.R. 2863 to the U.S. Senate by voice vote. The two approved changes increased the penalty provisions of the Migratory Bird Treaty Act and required a report on the general practice of baiting. When the bill reached the floor of the U.S. Senate it was incorporated within H.R. 2807, the Rhino and Tiger Product Labeling Act. Jim Saxton of New Jersey had sponsored this measure. This omnibus proposal had become a vehicle for modifications to the Migratory Bird Treaty Act; the National Wildlife Refuge System; the North American Wetlands Conservation Act; the Rhinoceros and Tiger Conservation Act; and the Chesapeake Bay System.

After both houses approved the legislation, President William J. Clinton signed it into law. In his signing statement, he said, "On balance, the Act provides a considerable benefit to the conservation of fish and wildlife, and I am pleased to sign it into law." Despite the strong objections of the Law Enforcement Division at the U.S. Fish and Wildlife Service, President Clinton made no mention of the elimination of strict liability. As Don Young had consistently emphasized, "This legislation will not allow baiting and will not imperil migratory bird populations. What it will do is allow hunters to simply present evidence in their own defense. As a footnote, it is my understanding that

177

there have been no charity dove hunts in Dixie County, Florida for the Florida Sheriffs Youth ranches since 1995.

In the final analysis, this was a remarkable legislative accomplishment for Don Young. He corrected a fundamental flaw in our judicial system for every migratory bird hunter without adversely affecting bird populations. Despite their loud protests, the U.S. Fish and Wildlife Service has for the past five years investigated and the courts have convicted numerous individuals in the 3,846 cases involving alleged violations of the Migratory Bird Treaty Act.

Public Law 105-312 was one of the most important landmark conservation measures approved during Don Young's Chairmanship and it would not have been possible without the dedication, leadership, and vision of the Congressman for All of Alaska.

When the gavel came down for the last time on October 4, 2000 at the end of the Full Resources Committee hearing on H.R. 4751, the Puerto Rico-United States Bilateral Pact of Non-Territorial Permanent Union and Guaranteed Citizenship Act, Don Young ended his Chairmanship with a smile of satisfaction on a job well done. If you listened closely, I am sure you could have heard Don Young humming the Frank Sinatra lyrics, "I've lived a life that's full, I traveled each and every highway.

But more, much more than this, I did it my
way!"

CHAPTER 7: CHAIRMAN OF TRANSPORTATION COMMITTEE

On January 3, 2001, Don Young became the first Alaskan Congressman to be elected Chairman of the Committee on Transportation and Infrastructure. While not an exclusive Committee like Energy and Commerce or Ways and Means, it is an important panel that has jurisdiction over our aviation system, federal public buildings, flood control, interstate highways, ports and waterways, railroads, and wastewater treatment plants.

Among the federal agencies it oversees are Amtrak, Appalachian Regional Commission, Federal Aviation Administration, Federal Emergency Management Agency, Federal Highway Administration, General Services Administration, U.S. Army Corps of Engineers, and the U.S. Coast Guard. As a result, legislation affecting our 926 coastal, Great Lakes, and inland harbors; 9,600 federal buildings; 19,700 civil airports; 138,000 miles of freight rail; and 4 million miles of public roads is referred to the Committee on Transportation and Infrastructure.

It is also an extremely important Committee to the more than 740,000 residents of the State of Alaska. These citizens depend upon and utilize Alaska's 482 airports including international hubs in Anchorage, Fairbanks, Juneau, and

Ketchikan; the 15,680 miles of interstate highways; the hundreds of miles of rail travel provided by the Alaska Railroad, the Pacific and Arctic Railway, and Navigation Company; and the thousands of jobs provided at the ports of Anchorage, Akutan, Dutch Harbor, Kodiak, Nikiski, and Valdez. It is essential that these facilities and roads are properly maintained and Don Young has always been committed to that effort.

By way of background, the Transportation and Infrastructure Committee, which was established in 1995, can trace its heritage back to the 14th Congress when the Roads and Canals Committee was established in 1831. Over the years, the name of the Committee has been changed to the Public Buildings and Grounds (1837), Rivers and Harbor Committee (1883), and the Committee on Public Works (1947). Don Young became the second Chairman of the newly constituted Committee that included new jurisdiction over the Federal Maritime Commission and the U.S. Coast Guard. Upon becoming Chairman in the 107th Congress, the Committee was the largest in the House. It had 59 members with 32 Republicans and 27 Democrats.

During his six years as Chairman, the Committee was not only popular but also highly productive. Between 2001 and 2006, 256 Transportation bills were passed by the House of Representatives and of that number, President George W. Bush signed 123 measures into law. Chairman Don Young sponsored 39 bills or 32 percent of the overall total. This success was a testament of Don Young's dedication, hard work, and leadership on behalf of this nation.

Among the Committee's key legislative achievements were the Aviation and Transportation Security Act of 2001 (P.L. 107-71), Railroad Retirement and Survivors Improvement Act (P.L. 107-90), John F. Kennedy Center for the Performing Arts Authorization Act (P.L. 107-224), Maritime Transportation Security Act (P.L. 107-295), the establishment of the Department of Homeland Security (P.L. 107-296), Flight 100 – Century of Aviation Reauthorization (P.L. 108-176), Safe, Accountable, Flexible, Efficient Transportation Equity Act: A Legacy for Users (P.L. 109-59), Katrina Emergency Assistance Act (P.L. 109-176), and the Pipeline Inspection, Protection, Enforcement and Safety Act (P.L. 109-468).

On September 11, 2001, we suffered one of the greatest tragedies in our history when 19 radical Islamic terrorists committed four coordinated attacks in this country. By hijacking four U.S. commercial planes, they murdered 2,996 people and injured more than 6,000. While none of the evil perpetrators survived the attacks, there was great concern about the failure of our national security agencies to detect and stop them.

The most common complaints were that the various national security agencies did not communicate with each other; there was a failure to share critical information, and an inability to connect the so-called dots. In order to avoid further terrorist attacks, a comprehensive review was immediately undertaken. A key recommendation was for the Congress to combine the various national security agencies within a new federal department.

On June 24, 2002, Majority Leader Dick Armey (R-TX) introduced the Homeland Security Act. This bill was referred to several House Committees including Transportation and Infrastructure. On July 11, 2002, that Committee met to consider H.R. 5005. The bill was reported favorably to the Select Committee on Homeland Security by voice vote with a number of important recommendations.

On July 19, 2002, the nine member Select Committee on Homeland Security met to consider the recommendations of 13 House standing Committees. After 18-recorded votes on amendments, the bill was favorably reported to the House of Representatives by a vote of 5 to 4. Voting for improved national security were Republicans Dick Armey, Tom Delay, J.C. Watts, Deborah Pryce, and Rob Porter. Voting NO were Democrats Nancy Pelosi, Martin Frost, Robert Menendez, and Rosa DeLauro.

As reported, H.R. 5005 created a new Department of Homeland Security to protect the security of the American people. According to the Committee report, "The Department will help fulfill the constitutional responsibility of the Federal government by providing for the common defense by uniting, under a single department those elements within the government whose primary responsibility is to secure the United States homeland. The Department will bring together 22 existing federal agencies or portion of agencies under a single clear chain of command."

Less than a week later, the House of Representatives considered the Homeland Security Act. In his opening statement, Majority Leader Dick Armey told his colleagues, "The world has changed. It is a much different world than it was in 1947 when the last transformation of our government took place. Our ability to deal with foreign terrorists remains limited. Many of our security resources are scattered, our technology is outdated, and the missions of our agencies on the front lines of terrorism are unfocused. Let us work together to make freedom secure as we cast our vote today."

For the next two days, the House spent more than sixteen hours debating 16 amendments offered by Republicans and Democrats. One of those amendments was offered by Don Young, which restored the Federal Emergency Management Agency

(FEMA) as an independent entity and maintained its role as the lead agency for the Federal Response Plan.

In his floor statement, the Chairman of the Transportation and Infrastructure Committee said, "I believe FEMA should stay intact as an entity so it can do the job people expect it to do, so it can do the job it has done and will continue to do the job under the Homeland Security bill." The Young Amendment was adopted by voice vote.

After disposing of the remaining amendments, the House voted 295 to 132 to better protect American citizens. After the Senate completed action, the House agreed to those modifications and the bill was presented to the White House. President George W. Bush signed the Homeland Security Act into law on November 25, 2002. In his signing statement, the President said, "We're fighting a new kind of war against determined enemies. This Administration and this Congress have the duty of putting that system into place. We will fulfill that duty. With the Homeland Security Act, we're doing everything we can to protect America. We're showing the resolve of this great nation to defend our freedom, our security, and our way of life."

As enacted in Public Law 107-296, this measure included a number of recommendations from the Transportation Committee. These included the

Transportation Security Administration keeping its status as a distinct entity; FEMA retained its core missions and responsibility as the lead agency for the Federal Response Plan; the Transportation Trust Funds were protected; and the Coast Guard was transferred to the Department of Homeland Security but was kept as a separate entity. In addition, incorporated within this law was Don Young's Arming Pilots Against Terrorism Act.

On January 24, 2003, former Pennsylvania Governor Thomas Ridge was sworn-in as the first Secretary of the newly created Department of Homeland Security (DHS). It was the 18th department established within the federal government.

In fiscal year 2004, DHS had more than 240,000 employees. This was the third largest number behind the Department of Defense (3 million) and the Department of Veterans Affairs (377,805). It has a budget of $40.6 billion, which was allocated to 22 federal agencies. These included: Federal Computer Incidence Response Center, Federal Emergency Management Agency, Federal Protective Service, Immigration and Naturalization Service, National Domestic Preparedness Office, Office of Domestic Preparedness, Transportation Security Administration, U.S. Coast Guard, and U.S. Customs Service.

In terms of aviation, for centuries man has looked up and marveled at the majesty of birds flying effortlessly in the sky. We have longed to join them in their peaceful pursuit. As Mark Twain wrote in *Roughing It*, "The air up there in the clouds is very pure and fine, bracing and delicious. And why shouldn't it be? It is the same air angels breathe."

At the turn of the 20th Century, two inventors from Dayton, Ohio, the Wright Brothers wrote to the U.S. Weather Bureau inquiring about a suitable place to conduct glider tests They were told that the hilly terrain, soft sand, wind, and remote location of Kitty Hawk, North Carolina made it an ideal location.

On the morning of December 17, 1903, these two young men made history by being the first to successfully fly a powered, heavier-than-air craft. The initial flight by Orville Wright lasted 12 seconds and traveled 120 feet. In his own words, he proclaimed, "The exhilaration of flying is too keen, the pleasure too great for it to be neglected as a sport."

At noon on that day, Wilbur Wright completed their fourth successful flight by traveling a record 852 feet over the course of 59 seconds. Upon completion of their epic adventure, the brothers sent a telegram to their father, Bishop Milton Wright that said, "Success. Four flights Thursday morning all against twenty-one mile wind. Started from level with engine power alone. Average speed through air thirty-one miles. Longest 57 seconds. Inform press. Home Christmas."

As someone who has stood in the very spot of that historic accomplishment, I can almost hear Wilbur Wright declaring to the world that, "If birds can glide for long periods of time, then why can't I." For the past 114 years, pilots throughout the world have been flying on the highways in the sky. We can thank Orville and Wilbur Wright for having the guts to follow their dream.

As a result of the 9/11 attacks and the threat of ongoing terrorism, the commercial airline industry faced a turbulent future. With declining air travel, higher security costs, and taxes, the industry lost $11.3 billion in 2002. With that backdrop, Don Young introduced H.R. 2115, the Vision 100 – Century of Aviation Reauthorization Act. It was referred exclusively to the Committee on Transportation and Infrastructure.

The bill was a tribute to the Wright Brothers and it was an effort to improve our aviation laws and revitalize our commercial airline industry. It was co-sponsored by the Committee's bipartisan leadership of John Mica (R-FL) James Oberstar (D-MN), and Peter DeFazio (D-OR).

The Subcommittee on Aviation conducted comprehensive public hearings on the Federal Aviation Administration's (FAA) Reauthorization. Subcommittee Chairman John Mica noted, "This legislation is critical to the future of aviation in our country. It is also fitting and I think very appropriate that on the 100th Anniversary of manned flight by the Wright brothers that we bring this rewrite of our federal aviation policy before the Congress. No nation in the world relies more on the safe and efficient operation of aircraft than the United States."

On May 14, 2003, the full Transportation and Infrastructure Committee reported H.R. 2115 by voice vote. In its Committee report, Chairman Young noted that, "The Committee strongly supports construction and improvements at all airports, not only the ones that qualify as congested. While most of the streamlining provisions of the bill focus on congested airports because of their impact on the national air transportation system, improvements at other airports are also important and should be encouraged."

On June 11, 2003, the House of Representatives considered the legislation. In his opening statement, Don Young said, "H.R. 2115 addresses the needs of the national aviation system today and in turn provides for the future. The Federal Aviation Administration oversees and ensures the safe and efficient use of our nation's airspace."

The Ranking Committee Democrat, James Oberstar added, "I, too, of course rise in support of H.R. 2115. When you think how far the world has come in aviation in just 100 years, it is really extraordinary. No other technology in the field of transportation can match the speed with which we have advanced the cause of aviation in this 100 years."

For the next five hours, the House considered five bipartisan amendments offered by John Mica, Eleanor Holmes Norton (D-DC), John Peterson (R-PA), Dan Manzullo (R-IL), and Joseph Pitts (R-PA). These measures affected the Buy America Act, the Metropolitan Washington Airports Authority, and small regional airports. They were all overwhelmingly adopted.

Prior to the vote on final passage of H.R. 2115, Don Young stated, "But nothing happens in this body without the cooperation from one another. I think this is an example of how Committees should work together in a bipartisan effort to achieve what is best for the nation as a whole." Clearly, the House agreed with that assessment because it voted 418 to 8 to approve the bill.

On June 12, 2003, the Senate debated the Aviation Investment and Reauthorization Vision Act. After disposing of 34 amendments, the members of the upper body approved the bill 94 to 0. For the next four months, a Conference Committee made up of representatives from both bodies considered the merits of the legislation.

On October 30, 2003, the House considered the Conference Report. Despite the fact that both bills explicitly barred the privatization of air traffic controllers, the Conference Report contained a provision strongly supported by the Bush Administration establishing an airport privatization pilot program. Democrat members were outraged. They refused to sign the Conference Report, argued against the provision and the process that resulted in its inclusion, and voted NO on final passage.

As someone who was involved in a number of Conference Committees, it was highly unusual to incorporate a provision that the House and Senate had rejected. The culprit was the Bush Administration who removed air traffic controllers from its definition of what constituted an inherently governmental function. This was a precursor to a privatization of the entire system. H.R. 2115 sought to prevent that effort by limiting the number of towers that could be privatized.

Prior to the final vote, Don Young reminded his colleagues that, "This industry has taken a tremendous beating. We need this legislation to pass. We need it to become law. We need to get on with the idea of making sure our airports are safe under this legislation, and that we have the ability to move passengers safely and on time. Overall, I believe it is a tremendous piece of legislation." Despite this articulate plea, the Conference Report was narrowly approved on a vote of 211 to 207. Almost a month later, the Senate adopted the Conference Report by voice vote.

On December 12, 2003, President George W. Bush signed H.R. 2115. In his signing statement, he noted that, "The act is designed to strengthen America's aviation sector, provide needed authority to the Federal Aviation Administration, and enhance the safety of the traveling public."

The major components of Public Law 108-176 were an authorization of $59 billion for airport planning and development grants; extended taxes on passenger tickets, freight, frequent flier awards, and aviation fuels; streamlined airport project reviews; extended federal war risk insurance for the airline industry; improved air service to isolated communities; extended the Small Community Air Service Development Program; authorized $483 million for the Essential Air Service Program; increased the number of slots at the Reagan National Airport; prohibited the closure of an airport without sufficient notice; airports in Alaska were not required to reduce the length of a runway; and allows flight crews to carry firearms to defend the cockpit.

In 2004, Don Young received the Aircraft Owners and Pilots Association's

(AOPA) most prestigious award. At the time it was awarded, AOPA President Phil Boyer stated, "Throughout his career on Capitol Hill, Rep. Young has shown a deep understanding of general aviation and has worked to ensure that GA remains a vital and integral part of the nation's aviation system."

It is now 14 years since the enactment of this important Don Young law. While air traffic control towers were not privatized, the Trump Administration has endorsed a plan to convert the existing air traffic control organization into a non-profit corporation governed by stakeholders.

In the 115th Congress, Bill Shuster the current Chairman of the Committee on Transportation and Infrastructure has introduced H.R. 2997, the 21st Century AIRR Act. A key component of this bill is to transfer the operation of air traffic services to a separate not-for-profit corporate entity. On June 27, 2017, the Committee voted to approve the bill with the transfer language by a vote of 32 to 25. There has been no further action scheduled in the House.

While the commercial airline industry has been experiencing record prosperity with $13.5 billion in profits in 2016, sadly, much of this has come at the expense of the flying public. Every day, airline passengers face persistent delays in service, unwanted invasions of their privacy, and endless fees on checked bags, blankets and pillows, in flight entertainment, meals, and seat selections. What was once a pleasurable experience has become a nightmare for many Americans. It is time for U.S. carriers to stop bragging about their profitability and to start caring about the millions of people who fly on their planes every year.

Like early air travel, those who could afford an automobile at the turn of the 20th Century were wealthy Americans. This changed in 1908, when Henry Ford of Detroit, Michigan started to mass-produce Model T cars for all Americans. They cost $825 dollars. While this was a lot of money, Henry Ford sold 15 million Model T's. Along with David Buick, Louis Chevrolet, Walter Chrysler, John Dodge, and Ramson Olds, these innovators changed America forever.

In 1910, the *Brooklyn Eagle* newspaper wrote that automobiling was, "The Last Call of the Wild." American poet Gertrude Tooley Buckingham opined that the, "Automobile is a joy, sublime. If you've enough gas and your tires are fine."

With the rapid growth of the U.S. automobile industry, Americans demanded the construction of highways to transport them to their doctors, their jobs, to visit family and friends or simply to explore sites in other cities during their leisure time. To satisfy that demand some of the most famous highways in America were built. These included U.S. Route 1, America's First Interstate Highway, U.S. Route 66 known as Will Rogers Highway or Main Street of America, and the Blue Ridge Parkway. These three highways, which are 2,369 miles, 2,448 miles, and 469 miles long, connected America from Maine to Florida, Chicago to California, and 29 North Carolina and Virginia counties.

Since it will take about 30 hours to drive from Chicago to Santa Monica on U.S. Route 66, motorists can enjoy the tasty fare at the Bobcat Bite or the Snow Cap Drive-In, visit Ed Galloway's Totem Pole Park, the Gemini Giant, or the Will Rogers Memorial Museum, or overnight at the Wigwam hotels.

For those leisurely driving on these three highways, there are hosts of interesting roadside attractions including the Biltmore Estate, Blowing Rock, Cadillac Ranch, Dinosaur Land, the Natural Bridge, Lost Sea, Luray Caverns, Ripley's Aquarium of the Smokies, and the Santa Monica Pier.

While each of these highways is historic, they were constructed before the establishment of the Federal Interstate Highway System. It is generally agreed that the birthplace of the interstate system was at the 46th Annual National Governor's Conference in Bolton Landing, New York. During that July 1954 Conference, Vice President Richard M. Nixon told the conferees that, "The federal government should take the lead in planning and building a modern highway system." The Vice President pledged that the Eisenhower Administration would spend up to $1 trillion for that effort.

In a February 22, 1955 message to the Congress, President Eisenhower, who is the father of the interstate system, stated, "I am inclined to the view that it is sounder to finance this program by special bond issues, to be paid off by the above mentioned revenues which will be collected during the useful life of the roads, rather than by an increase in general revenue obligations."

One year later, the U.S. Congress approved the landmark National Interstate and Defense Highways Act of 1956 (P.L. 84-627) that committed the federal government to paying 90 percent of the costs of a national system of super highways. The law authorized $25 billion to be spent over a ten-year period to build 41,000 miles of interstate highways. At the time, it was the largest public works project in American history. The first contract was signed on August 13, 1956 for the construction of U.S. 40 in the State of Missouri.

Thirty-five years later, the interstate highway system was declared completed. The final project was the opening of I-70 through Glenwood Canyon in Colorado. This job featured 40 bridges, numerous tunnels, and one of the most expensive rural highways per mile built in the United States. The total cost of the Dwight D. Eisenhower National System of Interstate and Defense Highways was $114 billion dollars.

During the past 25 years, the Congress has approved and Presidents have signed five major highway bills. These include the Intermodal Surface Transportation Efficiency Act of 1991 (ISTEA), the Transportation Equity Act for 21st Century Act of 1998 (TEA-21), Safe, Accountable, Flexible, Efficient Transportation Equity Act: A Legacy for Users Act of 2005 (SAFETEA-LU), Moving Ahead for Progress in the 21st Century Act of 2012 (MAP-21), and Fixing America's Surface Transportation Act of 2015 (FAST ACT).

These bills are popular with members of Congress because they offer a representative the opportunity to improve bridges, highways, and mass transit systems within their district. A five-year highway bill is a huge investment in our nation's surface transportation system, and it fosters job growth across the country. In fact, the Department of Transportation has estimated that for every $1 billion spent in highway funding, 47,500 jobs are created.

It was a three years process to enact SAFETEA-LU, which was named after the Chairman's beloved wife, Lu Young. On January 3, 2005, Don Young introduced the legislation and admonished his colleagues that, "Let's get the job done, so that our nation's commerce can move quickly and efficiently, commuters can get to work faster and easier, waste less gas sitting in traffic, and spend more time with their families. States, communities, and workers are waiting for us to act on this reauthorization."

H.R. 3 was substantially the same bill that passed the House by a vote of 357 to 65 on April 2, 2004. At the time it was proposed, there had been six short-term extensions of the various highway programs. The sixth expired on May 31, 2005. There would be an additional six extensions before SAFETEA-LU was signed into law.

On March 5, 2005, the House began consideration of H.R. 3. As the bill's author, Don Young began the debate by stating, "I have been Chairman of the Committee on Transportation and Infrastructure for the last 4 years. These 4 years have convinced me that we face a crisis in this country because of our inadequate, crumbling, and congested highways."

Don Young met with dozens of members of the House who were interested in having their highway projects incorporated within his bill. As a result of these discussions, 3,315 high priority projects in all 50 states plus the District of Columbia, American Samoa, and Puerto Rico were incorporated within SAFETEA-

LU. Of this total, 19 projects were in Alaska with an authorization of $77 million. These included badly needed efforts to fix access roads in Fairbanks, Juneau, North Pole and Williamsport, the ferry terminals in Kodiak and Unalaska, the Knik Arm Bridge, and the Seward Highway.

There was overwhelmingly support for this legislation. The Ranking Democrat of the Committee, Jim Oberstar said, "The gentleman from Alaska has led us through political storms over this issue. He has been a steady hand at the helm, and I applaud his leadership and fairness." Hal Rogers (R-KY), a senior member of the Appropriations Committee noted that, "This is a job bill, a security bill and most importantly, a life saving bill." Jimmy Duncan (R-TN) a senior member of the Transportation Committee told the House, "This is the biggest job bill we will vote on in this Congress. If you believe in job growth, safer highways, less congestion and a strong America, then you should vote for this bill."

Praise for the bill and its author was not limited to members of his own party, Eleanor Holmes Norton said, "I begin by thanking the leadership of this Committee, which is a real model for bipartisan leadership. They know how to get the job done. I hope the Congress finally follows suit." The Ranking Democrat on the Highway Subcommittee, Peter DeFazio noted, "I, believe, this may be the signature accomplishment of this Congress."

During the next two days, the House considered 40 bipartisan amendments. After debating each proposed change to H.R. 3, the House voted 417 to 9 to approve the legislation. On May 17, 2005, the U.S. Senate voted 89 to 11 in favor of the measure. After a successful Conference to resolve the various differences, the House gave its final approval to SAFETEA-LU on July 29, 2005 by a vote of 412 to 8. Prior to voting, Don Young stated, "H.R. 3 provides a funding level of $286.45 billion in guaranteed funding over 6 years for federal highways and transit programs, as well as highway safety and motor carrier safety programs. I especially want to thank the gentleman from Minnesota, Mr. Oberstar, who has been unwavering in his support and working in cooperation with this Chairman."

The Senate concurred on July 9, 2005 by a vote of 91 to 4. President George W. Bush signed the 836-page bill into law on August 10, 2005. In his signing statement, the President noted, "Today, I have signed into law H.R. 3, the Safe, Accountable, Flexible, Efficient Transportation Equity Act: A Legacy for Users. The Act is designed to improve the nation's highway safety, modernize roads, reduce traffic congestion, and create jobs."

There were a number of key provisions contained within Public Law 109-59. These included an investment of $246.9 billion, an extension of highway user taxes, and the maintenance of the 46,000-mile interstate system. Specifically, $52 billion was authorized for transit programs; $32.5 billion for the surface transportation program; $30.5 billion for the National Highway System; $25 billion for the interstate highway maintenance program; $21 billion for the highway bridge and maintenance program; $8.6 billion to ease traffic congestion; and $5 billion for the highway safety improvement program.

The writing of a five-year highway bill is a massive undertaking. In the case of H.R. 3, it required 11 extensions, member discussions, and the bipartisan cooperation of Don Young, James Oberstar, John Mica and Peter DeFazio. As the sponsor, Don Young was the conductor, facilitator, and glue that kept the process moving forward.

SAFETEA-LU was the largest surface transportation investment in our nation's history. It put to work thousands of Americans, improved highway safety, replaced unsafe bridges, resulted in the construction of thousands of high priority projects, and saved thousands of American lives. As a young man, Don Young worked in construction in Alaska. H.R. 3 was his greatest construction job and it is a tribute to his tireless leadership on behalf of the American people.

CHAPTER 8: DEAN OF THE HOUSE

On December 5, 2017, Don Young became the 13th Republican and 48th overall Dean of the House of Representatives. By becoming the longest serving member in the 115th Congress, he joined an illustrious group of legislators including John Quincy Adams, Sam Rayburn, and John Dingell.

The practice of acknowledging the most senior member has its roots in the English Parliament. However, the term Dean of the House was not originally used. Instead, the first Dean was called the "Father of the House." The first Speaker of the House Frederick Muhlenberg was sworn-in by New York Supreme Court Chief Justice Richard Morris in 1789. This was the only time in U.S. history that a non-House member administered the oath.

While largely a ceremonial position, whose primary responsibility is to swear-in the Speaker of the House; Don Young has remained steadfast in his commitment to the citizens of Alaska. For the first time in a decade, Republicans control both the Executive and Legislative branches of our government.

One of the new Congress' first tasks was to review certain regulations issued by the Obama Administration. During his eight years, Barack Obama signed more than 600 major regulations, costing $743 billion, and requiring 194 million hours to complete the necessary paperwork requirements. This was a huge increase over his predecessors and many of these new regulations had a devastating effect on our economy.

In order to review these regulations, Republicans utilized the authority of the Congressional Review Act of 1996 (P.L. 104-21). Under this law, the 115th Congress was able to overturn any major rule submitted on or after June 13, 2016 by a simple majority vote in both houses.

During the first 20 years of Public Law 104-21, the Congress was successful only once in March 2001 when it eliminated the Clinton's Administration's Department of Labor rule on ergonomics. During the 115th Congress, 15 disapproval resolutions were approved and signed into law by President Donald J. Trump. These erased rules affecting abortions, education, environment, financial issues, gun rights, Internet privacy, labor, and wildlife management.

One of the successfully overturned rules was one issued by the Department of the Interior entitled, "Non-subsistence take of Wildlife and Public Participation and Closure Procedures, on National Wildlife Refuges in Alaska. According to the U.S. Fish and Wildlife Service the, "Rule will help facilitate the ability of the Service to maintain sustainable populations of bears, wolves, and coyotes throughout national wildlife refuges across Alaska." Specifically, the rule restricted certain hunting practices on Alaska's national wildlife refuges including aerial shooting, baiting, and trapping.

Since the founding of our Republic, states and not the federal government have had primacy over wildlife within their state including those residing on federal lands. This new rule, which became effective on September 6, 2016, seized authority to manage fish and wildlife from the State of Alaska. It is my view that this rule violated the Alaska Constitution, the Alaskan Statehood Act, the Alaska National Interest Lands Conservation Act of 1980, and the National Wildlife Refuge System Improvement Act of 1997. Section 8 of the 1997 law specifically stated that, "Nothing in this Act shall be constructed as affecting the authority, jurisdiction, or responsibility of the several states to manage, control, or regulate fish and resident wildlife under state law or regulations in any area within the system."

On January 13, 2017, the State of Alaska filed suit in the United States District Court for the District of Alaska against then Department of the Interior Secretary Sally Jewell. In its 47-page legal brief, the state argued that, "It is well established that the power to manage and protect wildlife, including on federal lands, lies with the state."

The submission also concluded that, "The FWS rule violates these provisions of the National Wildlife Refuge System

Improvement Act and specifically interferes with Alaska's authority to manage, control, and regulate wildlife." The rule promulgated by the U.S. Fish and Wildlife Service affected all 16 wildlife refuges in Alaska, which comprise 76.8 million acres or nearly 20 percent of the state.

On February 7, 2017, Don Young introduced House Joint Resolution 69 (H.J. Res). The purpose of this legislation was to disapprove the rule and declare that it had no force or effect. This measure was strongly supported by the State of Alaska, the entire Alaskan Congressional delegation, all the elected officials in the State of Alaska, and more than 20 conservation and hunting organizations. This list included the Association of Fish and Wildlife Agencies, Congressional Sportsmen's Foundation, Ducks Unlimited, National Rifle Association, Sportsmen's Alliance, and Wildlife Management Institute.

On February 16, 2017, the House considered H. J. Res. 69. As the sponsor, Don Young told his colleagues, "H. J. Res. 69 is very simple. It overturns an illegal rule by the Obama Administration. This House created the State of Alaska in 1959 under the Statehood Act. It clearly granted Alaska full authority to manage fish and game on all lands in the State of Alaska, including all federal lands." At the end of the debate, the House voted 225 to 193 to disapprove this rule that infringed on a state's ability to manage fish and wildlife.

On March 21, 2017, the Senate voted 52 to 47 to reject the Fish and Wildlife Service's September 2016 rule. In her statement, Senator Lisa Murkowski noted that, "Congress explicitly provided Alaska with the authority to manage its fish and wildlife in not one, not two, but three separate laws – the Alaska Statehood Act, ANILCA, and the National Wildlife Refuge System Administration Act. The Fish and Wildlife Service rule is bad for Alaska, bad for hunters, bad for our native peoples, and bad for America."

On April 3, 2017, President Donald J. Trump signed the legislation into law. Upon its signing, Don Young said, "Upholding the rule of law and protecting Alaska's authority to manage fish and game throughout our state is critically important to me – which is why I worked tirelessly to eliminate this unlawful rule. It's important to note that this resolution does not allow for brutal, inhumane or unsporting hunting practices." Under terms of the Congressional Review Act of 1996, any rule wiped off the books cannot be reinstated by any federal agency in a "substantially similar" form.

In 1992, the Congress enacted the Indian Employment, Training, and Related Services Demonstration Act (P.L. 102-477). Under this law, tribal governments were allowed to consolidate up to 13 different programs administered by the Departments of Education, Health and Human Services, Interior, and Labor into a single plan. These 477 Plans, which are approved by the Department of the Interior, are designed to foster economic development and employment in Indian Country. The 477 Program provides flexibility to tribal governments to create employment, training, and economic development plans that utilize money from several federal programs to meet the needs of local communities. While it is still a "demonstration project," 265 tribes have consolidated multiple federal programs into a single 477 Plan for the benefit of their members. In fiscal year 2014, these tribes received more than $90 million in grant funding.

For the past two Congresses, Don Young has introduced legislation to make 477 Plans permanent, to increase the availability of federal grant programs, streamline the review process, and improve the program's accounting procedures, administration, and efficiency. By so doing, more critical dollars can be allocated to the participating tribes. In 2017, the Natural Resources Committee favorably reported H.R. 228, the Young bill, by voice vote.

On February 27, 2017, Don Young stipulated on the floor of the House of Representatives that, "The 477 Program has a proven track record of success and allows for bold approaches to address significant education and training needs that exist in Indian country. This program is what tribal self-determination is all about. Tribes understand their members best and know how to use these tools for creating and expanding employment opportunities in their communities."

Prior to the unanimous House passage of H.R. 228, the Ranking Democrat on the Natural Resources Subcommittee on Indian, Insular and Alaska Native Affairs, Norma Torres (D-CA) said, "I want to congratulate Chairman Young for his tireless work on this legislation and for bringing together all of the stakeholders to address their concerns and finding a workable solution."

On November 29, 2017, the U.S. Senate passed H.R. 228 without amendments by unanimous consent. President Donald J. Trump signed this important legislation into law on December 18, 2017. It is now Public Law 115-93.

As someone who was married to an Alaskan native for 46 years and taught at a Bureau of Indian Affairs school in Fort Yukon, Don Young has always been an advocate for Alaska's 229 recognized tribes and the Alaskan native people.

In Alaska there is a small community living in King Cove that has been seeking relief from the federal government for nearly 40 years.

Archaeological evidence has proven that Aleut people have lived there for at least 4,000 years. King Cove is named after the first recorded settler, Robert King, who moved there in the early 1800's. The village is located between two volcanic mountains near the end of the Alaska Peninsula.

Since the early 1980's, the residents of King Cove have tried to obtain a safe and dependable transportation access for their severely sick residents to the airport in Cold Bay, Alaska.

Today, there are about 1,000 people living on 16,308 acres of land, which is 625 miles southwest of Anchorage. King Cove has a small clinic that is not a trauma center and a 1,600-foot gravel airstrip. During the long winter months, harsh weather and gale-force winds close the airport more than 100 days each year. Flights are routinely delayed because of severe weather.

As a result of these weather conditions, Native Americans are prevented from accessing hospitals and other emergency services. Sadly, one 70-year old resident had a major heart attack but had to wait three days at the King Cove clinic before being evacuated to a trauma center. Eighteen residents have died including some in fatal air crashes.

The Alaska Congressional delegation has long supported a 11-mile one-lane gravel road that would connect existing roads on both sides of the Izembek National Wildlife Refuge. As an alternative to this vital road, the delegation was successful in obtaining $37 million to construct a hovercraft terminal. This option proved to be a failure because of huge operating costs and an inability to utilize the hovercraft in rough weather. The service was terminated in 2010.

In 2009, the delegation was successful in having language incorporated within the Omnibus Parks Land Management Act (P.L. 111-11). Specifically, the Secretary of Interior was directed to determine whether a land exchange with the State of Alaska was in the public interest. Under the terms of such an exchange, the State of Alaska would receive 206 acres of federal lands in return for surrendering title to thousands of acres of state lands.

On December 13, 2013, Secretary Jewell announced that a road through the Izembek National Wildlife Refuge would not be in the national interest. During her visit to King Cove in August 2013, she told the residents that she was there to "Speak on behalf of the Izembek birds and animals, which have no voice."

What a disgraceful and insensitive comment. This road, which will have no impact on wildlife, is certainly in the interests of the people of King Cove whose ancestors have lived on this land for over

4,000 years. It is certainly in the interests of a resident who goes into premature labor, breaks a leg, or suffers a severe heart attack or stroke whose only hope for survival is a safe transport to the Cold Bay Airport. Since the Secretary's visit, there have been 68 medevacs out of King Cove. The U.S. Coast Guard was able to provide assistance to some of these critically ill Americans.

The Izembek National Wildlife Refuge was established by the Eisenhower Administration in 1960 with the signing of Public Land Order 2216. It is comprised of about 315,000 acres most of which was declared wilderness in 1980. Under the Wilderness Act of 1964 (P.L. 88-577), a wilderness is an area "where the earth and its community of life are untrammeled by man, where man himself is a visitor who does not remain." Based on that definition, Izembek does not qualify for wilderness status even after the Fish and Wildlife Service burned down subsistence cabins in the 1980's. This area was an Air Force base during World War II. The Air Force constructed in Cold Bay an all-weather 10,180-foot airstrip, which is the fourth longest paved runway in the State. Within the refuge there are 78 miles of roads, which supplied the military base. King cove residents are seeking to build a road on the edge of the refuge, which would be 2 miles from the sensitive Izembek lagoon.

While Secretary Jewell suggested there are other alternatives, each of these have been examined and rejected. The hovercraft experiment failed. It is extremely difficult, if not impossible, to either fly or transport by boat a critically injured or sick King Cove resident, in their harsh weather conditions. These people are literally risking their lives on a daily basis.

Sadly, Secretary Jewell ignored the pleas of desperate King Cove residents and listened to the voices of radical environmental groups who care far more about birds than human beings. These organizations have proven time and again that they don't care whether King Cove Native Americans live or die.

In the current Congress, Don Young re-introduced the King Cove Road Land Exchange Act. Under the terms of H.R. 218, the State of Alaska would receive 206 acres of federal lands for an 11-mile gravel road. In return, the state would transfer title to 43,093 acres to the Department of the Interior. This is a more than a 200 to 1 land exchange and the proposed corridor is 0.06 percent of the refuge.

On April 5, 2017, the Natural Resources Subcommittee on Federal Lands held a hearing on H.R. 218. At that time, Della Trumble a spokesperson for the King Cove Community testified that, "Please know we will never quit fighting until we are successful in our quest to achieve a safe, dependable and affordable transportation solution for our residents. We know the only logical solution is a modest, non-invasive, one-lane gravel road. Finally, we are so fortunate to have Congressman Young's commitment, common sense, and passion to help us achieve this solution."

On July 20, 2017, the House considered the King Cove Road Lane Exchange Act. During the debate, Don Young noted, "Now some people will say. Well, they have got an airport. Yes. 1,600 feet. Winds are blowing 90 miles an hour. You try to get off. Or put yourself on a boat and go across in 30-foot waves. We had one lady evacuated at a cost of $250,000 by the Coast Guard. The helicopter crashed, and she lost her life. We had two other elders that went across in a crab boat. They had to put the people into a crab pot because there was no other way to get to this airport."

He concluded by saying, "I am suggesting to my colleagues, let's do what is right. This does no harm to the refuge. It saves lives, gives them an opportunity to take and experience the medical care that all the rest of us have. Let's do the right thing today."

After rejecting several mean spirited amendments, the House voted 248 to 179 to approve the bill. There were 16 Democrat members including the entire Hawaiian delegation who bravely voted for this legislation. I say bravely because they now risk the wrath of the environmental community who are willing to spend millions to destroy those members who dare to disagree with their radical agenda.

After its passage, Don Young said, "This is truly an issue of life or death for the residents of the isolated community of King Cove. The people of King Cove have fought for over 30 years for safe and reliable access to emergency care and it is past time we make it a reality. Frankly, I will not rest until we do."

While the U.S. Senate could certainly consider the Young bill, passage in that body is unlikely because of the 60-vote requirement. As an alternative, the Agdaagux and Belkofski tribes and the Alaska Congressional Delegation have been actively seeking a land exchange with the Department of the Interior.

On January 22, 2018, Secretary of the Interior Ryan Zinke signed an agreement with the King Cove Corporation to begin the process of building the 11-mile road to Cold Bay Airport. Under the terms of this agreement, both sides stipulated that any land exchange would be of equal value, it would not exceed 500 acres, the road would be a two-way, single-lane gravel road, it shall be used primarily for health, safety and quality of life purposes, time is of the essence to complete the land exchange, and the agreement will expire on December 31, 2027.

In signing the agreement for the United States, Secretary Zinke said, "Above all, the federal government's job is to keep our people safe and respect our treaty commitments with Native Americans and Alaska natives. Today I am proudly fulfilling both of those missions."

Della Trumble, spokeswoman for the King Cove Corporation responded, "Access to the all-weather airport in Cold Bay is truly a matter of life and death to us. Today's agreement goes a long way toward restoring our faith that the federal government takes seriously its trust responsibility to the Aleut and to all Alaska Natives."

In his statement to the press, Don Young said, "I have been working with the residents of King Cove for over 30 years to help them get a life-saving road to the community of Cold Bay. This is a great day not only for King Cove but also for all of Alaska. In 2013, Sally Jewell decided that birds are more important than people, and today we finally have a Secretary who takes the life and death of Alaska Natives seriously. I want to thank Secretary Zinke on behalf of all Alaskans for his work in getting the King Cove road approved."

In the United States, hydroelectric power is one of the oldest methods of producing power. In the first hydroelectric power was generated at a plant in Grand Rapids, Michigan. The year was 1880 and the power was used to light 16 streetlights. A year later, hydroelectricity produced lights that illuminated Niagara Falls for tourists.

Today, hydroelectric power is the most widely used renewable source of energy. In 2015, these power stations produced 35 percent of the total renewable electricity in the United States. This 101,000 megawatts of power represented about 6 percent of the nation's total electricity. For every one-megawatt of electricity created 750 to 1,000 American homes are powered.

In the State of Alaska, there are 34 hydroelectric facilities. They produce 423 megawatts or 21 percent of the state's electrical energy. The five largest facilities are located at Bradley Lake, Snettisham Lake, Swan Lake, Eklutna Lake, and Terror Lake. Within Alaska there is a potential for huge increases in hydroelectric power, which is reliable, inexpensive to operate and maintain, renewable, and reduce greenhouse gas emissions.

In an effort to promote this safe and reliable source of energy, Don Young introduced a bill to expand the Terror Lake hydroelectric project on Kodiak Island, Alaska. The Federal Energy Regulatory Commission (FERC) licensed this project in 1981. It currently produces 31 megawatts of power for the 13,789 residents of the island and the largest Coast Guard station in the United States.

Under H.R. 220, the Kodiak Electric Company, which operates the plant, would be allowed to divert additional water from the Upper Hidden Basin into Terror Lake by digging a 1.5-mile underground tunnel. In addition, the bill clarifies that this expansion will not require a revised FERC license nor will it affect the ability of the Fish and Wildlife Service to impose conditions on that license. This language is necessary to ensure the timely expansion of this project and to safeguard the federal government's fiduciary responsibility to protect the Kodiak Island National Wildlife Refuge, which is the site of the hydroelectric project.

H.R. 220 was reported unanimously from the Natural Resources Committee. It was considered in the House on June 27, 2017. At that time, the author Don Young said, "This diversion will increase the water resources at Terror Lake by 25 percent resulting in an additional 33,000 mega-watt-hours of generation each year. Alaska has tremendous hydroelectric potential and I look forward to moving additional commonsense reforms to provide our rural and remote communities with new opportunities to obtain reliable and affordable hydropower." When the roll was called, H.R. 220 passed on a vote of 424 to 1. Since the U.S. Senate approved this legislation during the previous

Congress, I am confident this measure will be signed into law.

On February 5, 2018, the House considered a second Young hydroelectric bill known as the Swan Lake Hydroelectric Project Boundary Correction Act. During debate, the Democrat floor manager Colleen Hanabusa (D-HI) said it best, "We all know that when it comes to Alaska, no one is a better advocate and the strongest proponent of what is right and for the State of Alaska than my good friend, the Representative from Alaska." This is high praise from a member of the opposing party and it speaks volumes of Don Young's commitment to bipartisan solutions and to the people of the great State of Alaska. The bill was approved by voice vote and hopefully the Senate will concur.

In 1971, the Alaska Native Claims Settlement Act extinguished all claims of the native peoples based on aboriginal title to lands and waters in Alaska. It also established a procedure whereby 25 or more native residents could form a village. By becoming an Alaskan native village the residents were entitled to a surface estate of between 69,120 and 161,280 acres depending upon its population size. Title II of Public Law 92-203 listed about 200 villages.

One of the communities examined for village designation was Alexander Creek. This community is 27 miles northwest of Anchorage. While Alexander Creek was given status, this administrative recognition was challenged in court and ultimately erroneously overturned by the Alaska Native Claims Appeal Board. For the past 40 years, this issue has been litigated and the residents of Alexander Creek have been denied the benefits they deserve.

On March 7, 2017, Don Young introduced H.R. 1418. Under this bill, Alexander Creek is formally recognized as a native village and within 13 months of the enactment of this law, the community will enter into a cooperative agreement with the Department of the Interior to "fairly and equitably settle aboriginal land claims."

On July 26, 2017, the Natural Resources Committee considered the legislation and favorably voted to send the measure to the House of Representatives by unanimous consent. During debate, Don Young told the Committee that, "For more than 45 years, families from Alexander Creek have lacked the foundation for social and economic support afforded to other villages. My bill would open a negotiation between Alexander Creek and the Department of the Interior to fairly and equitably settle Alexander Creek's claims. My bill does not prescribe any benefits but ensures that the settlement will be right value parity with other corporations giving consideration for the time that has passed since the Alaska

Native Claims Settlement Act. It takes care of an injustice that occurred in 1971." I fully expect that H.R. 1418 will pass the House of Representatives in the near future.

While it takes a matter of days for a private company to obtain a federal permit to build a wind turbine or energy project, it takes years for an Indian tribe or Alaskan Native Corporation to obtain the identical permission. This is fundamentally wrong.

In 1982, the Congress approved the Indian Land Mineral Leasing Act. Under this law, a tribe or native corporation may only lease their trust lands for mineral development "subject to the approval of the Secretary." This approval is contingent on satisfying the requirements of the National Environmental Policy Act and its myriad of appraisals, permit applications, and endless reviews involving multiple federal agencies. The net result is costly and unnecessary delays.

On June 15, 2015, the Government Accountability Office (GAO) issued a report entitled, *Indian Energy Development. Poor Management by BIA has Hindered Energy Development on Indian Lands."* What this comprehensive report found was that it takes an inordinate amount of time to review and issue a permit for energy development in Indian county. For instance, GAO stated that it takes three years to approve a utility scale wind project, five years to review pipeline agreements, and eight years to issue permits to the Southern Ute Indian Tribe. The consequences of these delays are financially huge. In the case of the Utes, these delays cost the tribe more than $95 million in lost revenues. These desperately needed funds were denied to local hospitals, law enforcement, and schools on their reservation.

On October 4, 2017, the Natural Resources Committee met to consider the Native American Energy Act. Under the Young bill, appraisals of Indian and Native Corporation lands could be conducted by the Secretary of the Interior, the tribe or corporation, or a certified third-part appraiser; any Environmental Impact Statement would be reviewed only by members of the Indian tribe or Native Corporation or individuals residing within the affected area; and the time for filings and lawsuits would be expedited. The fundamental goal is to streamline the permitting, leasing, and development of energy projects.

Sadly, Democrats on the Committee opposed the legislation because they were more interested in protecting the National Environmental Policy Act (NEPA) rather than help America's native people. During my career on Capitol Hill, I witnessed this attitude on numerous occasions. I firmly believe that we could not today build the Alaska pipeline, the interstate highway system, or the Pentagon because of those who blindly adhere to NEPA.

During the debate, Don Young articulated his commitment, frustration, and passion for all native people. In one of his finest statements, he said, "This bill was written by the natives themselves. I am tired of the other side patting him on the head my American natives and saying we support you and handing him a blanket and a side of beef. And that is what you have done. You have not encouraged their advancement at all."

He went on to say, "They have been told it takes three years to get a permit to do something on a reservation and two days to get it on private land. This constant progressive liberal approach saying we are helping the poor is nonsense. You want to keep them down. You don't want them to have their own way to fund their own careers, their own lives, and their own reservations. You want to pat them on the head. I have lived with the natives most of my life and watched the government in what they have done. The unemployment, the drugs, the drunkenness's, and the violence are all created because of the progressive attitude we will take care of you. All this bill does is to give them an opportunity – not to destroy the environment – but in fact the right to move their resources faster or as fast as private landowners."

At the conclusion of this powerful speech, the Committee voted 25 to 15 to approve H.R. 210. In his press release, Don Young opined, "The Native American Energy Act is critically important to Alaska Natives and American Indians because it levels the playing field for responsible resource development, an essential step towards self-determination."

I expect the House of Representatives will approve H.R. 210 largely along partisan political lines. Its fate in the U.S. Senate is far less certain.

Finally, on December 13, 2017, the House Natural Resources Committee favorably reported H.R. 200, H.R. 4475, and H.R. 1901, which were sponsored by Don Young. Of these bills, the most comprehensive was H.R. 200, the Strengthening Fishery Communities and Increased Flexibility Management Act. This measure updates and improves our nation's premier fisheries law, the Magnuson-Stevens Fishery Conservation and Management Act. In fact, it carries the same bill number that was signed into law on April 13, 1976 by President Gerald Ford.

After being favorably reported on a 23 to 17 vote, Don Young opined, "My bill updates the Magnuson-Stevens Act (MSA) to ensure regional fisheries are able to develop management plans that match the needs of areas which they know best. MSA has not been reauthorized since 2006, it is long past time for this Congress to pass and support our nation's fisheries." I expect the House of Representatives will approve H.R. 200 in 2018.

The second bill was H.R. 4475. Under this legislation, the United States Geological Service (USGS) is directed to establish the National Volcano Early Warning and Monitoring System. Under this program, USGS would issue warnings, monitor geological data, and protect U.S. citizens from volcanic activity. Since this bill was favorably reported by unanimous consent, it is likely to be approved by the full House in 2018.

The third Young bill was H.R. 1901. This proposal directs the Secretary of Health and Human Services to convey 19 acres of federal land to the Southeast Alaska Regional Health Consortium. This consortium that serves Alaskan natives across the state covers more than 35,000 square miles; affects 28 community health clinics, and the Mt. Edgecumbe Hospital in Sitka. The Senate version S. 825 was adopted by unanimous consent on November 30, 2017. I fully expect the House will approve the measure.

At the end of the 1st Session of the 115th Congress, the new Dean of the House of Representatives was successful in having three of his bills signed into law, two additional measures approved by the House, and five more bills awaiting House

225

debate. This is a tremendous record of achievement for a single legislative year.

CHAPTER 9: ANWR'S COASTAL PLAIN

For over 10,000 years, the Inupiat Eskimo people of Kaktovik have lived and survived by utilizing the abundant natural resources of the Coastal Plain. For generations these proud semi-nomadic people have harvested fish, fur, game, and marine mammals. These resources have provided the very necessities of their life.

The name Kaktovik means a "Large pond of good fresh water on high ground." The approximately 250 Inupiat residents live on Barter Island located within the Arctic National Wildlife Refuge. The community is 855 miles north of Anchorage, 150 miles above the Arctic Circle, and 90 miles west of the Canadian border. It is the most northern village in North America. The residents depend on the bowhead whale, Dall sheep, fish, and muskoxen for their nutritional needs.

On December 6, 1960, Secretary of the Interior Fred A. Seaton issued Public Land Order 2214. The net effects of this administrative action were the establishment of the Arctic National Wildlife Range and the withdrawal of 8.9 million acres from all forms of use. Prior to becoming Secretary, Seaton represented the State of Nebraska in the U.S. Senate, was a special White House advisor to President Dwight D. Eisenhower, and visited Alaska on several occasions. During one of those visits, he described the new 49th state as "One of the world's great wildlife areas."

Public Land Order 2214 remained in effect until December 2, 1980, when President Jimmy Carter signed into law the Alaska Lands Interest Conservation Act. Under the provisions of Public Law 96-487, 19 million acres were incorporated within the newly named Arctic National Wildlife Refuge (ANWR), the largest wilderness area was created on the North Slope, and the future of the 1.5 million acre Coastal Plain was left for further Congressional action.

Specifically, Section 1002 states that, "The purpose of this section was to provide for a comprehensive and continuing inventory and assessment of the fish and wildlife resources of the Coastal Plain; an analysis of the impacts of oil and gas exploration, development, and production; and an estimate of how much oil and gas may exist under the 1002 area. The first inventory report was due to the U.S. Congress no later than December 1985. However, Section 1003 of Public Law 96-487 says, "No leasing or other development leading to production of oil and gas from the range shall be undertaken until authorized by an Act of Congress."

On August 18, 1980, Senator Paul Tsongas (D-MA) an author of the Alaska National Interest Lands Conservation Act, stated on the Senate floor that, "With regard to the Arctic Range, this substitute would designate the entire range, exclusive of most of the Coastal Plain, as wilderness. I remain concerned about oil exploration in the Coastal Plain of the Arctic Range, and I hope the advocates of that program are correct that seismic work can be done without adverse impact." The bottom line is that the Coastal Plain is not and never has been a wilderness area.

On April 20, 1987, Secretary of Interior Don Hodel released the "Arctic National Wildlife Refuge, Alaska, Coastal Plain Resource Assessment and Legislative Environmental Impact Statement Report" as required by Section 1002. A key finding of that report was that the entire 1.5 million acres of the Coastal Plain should be open to oil and gas leasing. This conclusion was prompted by the Department's seismic exploration program. Over the course of two winter seasons, the Department completed over 1,300 miles of seismic survey work.

In the Department's Press Release, Secretary Hodel stated, "Geologists consider the ANWR Coastal Plain the most outstanding onshore frontier area for prospective major oil discoveries in America. These potentially vast oil resources would provide tremendous economic benefits to our country. Our nation has proven that we need not choose between exploring for and developing the energy necessary for survival and growth on one hand, and protecting the environment on the other, we can have both."

As a result of this report, the House Merchant Marine and Fisheries Committee began a series of hearings on whether to authorize exploration in the 1002 area. At one of those hearings, Don Young implored his Committee colleagues to, "Let the public make up their minds with the honest facts not myth or fantasyland." What he was referencing was a picture that was to appear in the National Audubon Society's monthly magazine. The picture alleged to depict the 1002 area, yet the Coastal Plain was nowhere in sight. For years, the environmental community intentionally misrepresented the Coastal Plain and referred to it as "America's Serengeti" or an untrammeled wilderness area. It is neither. The Coastal Plain is flat, treeless, and frozen arctic tundra. It has been described as an Arctic desert. Interestingly, in the mid-1970's, environmental groups urged the Congress to build the Alaskan pipeline through ANWR because in their opinion there were no important environmental features in the region. This did not, however, stop these organizations from raising millions of dollars based on false, misleading, and wrong characterizations of the Coastal Plain of ANWR.

At the conclusion of the Committee hearings, the Merchant Marine and Fisheries Committee favorably reported H.R. 3601, the National Fish and Wildlife

Enhancement Act by a vote of 28 to 13. The Chairman of the Committee, Walter B. Jones, Sr. (D-NC) had introduced the bill. The purpose of the legislation was, "to authorize and direct the Secretary of the Interior to initiate an oil and gas leasing program for the coastal plain of the Arctic National Wildlife Refuge. In its Committee Report, Chairman Jones concluded that, "The North Slope of Alaska and the Coastal Plain of ANWR have been recognized for a number of years as areas with excellent potential for large oil and gas reserves."

At the same time, the Senate Energy and Natural Resources Committee favorably reported S. 2214, the Arctic Coastal Plain Competitive Oil and Gas Leasing Act. The Committee Chairman J. Bennett Johnston (D-LA) sponsored the bill. According to the Committee Report 100-308, "The purpose of this measure is to authorize and direct the Secretary of the Interior to establish and implement a competitive oil and gas leasing program for the Coastal Plain of the Arctic National Wildlife Refuge." It went on to say, "The Coastal Plain is a particularly promising area for oil and gas. For years, this area has been rated by many geologists as the most outstanding target in the onshore United States."

During the 100th Congress, there were 35 hearings and mark-ups on the Coastal Plain of ANWR. These occurred in the House Interior and Insular Affairs

Committee, the House Merchant Marine and Fisheries Committee, and the Senate Energy and Natural Resources Committee. Despite legislative momentum, there was no further Congressional action on H.R. 3601 or S. 2214. Nevertheless, it was clear that these two prominent Democrat Chairmen were convinced that it was time to develop the Coastal Plain in an environmentally safe manner. They also understood that these potential oil and gas resources were essential to our national security and energy independence.

Sadly, before any further action in the 101st Congress, the oil tanker *Exxon Valdez* struck Bligh Reef on March 29, 1989. This environmental catastrophe caused the spilling of 10.8 million gallons of unrefined crude oil into the pristine Prince William Sound in Alaska. It caused the killing of fish, livelihoods, wildlife, and the opportunity to explore the ANWR Coastal Plain.

Although statistics have proven that oil tankers cause far more environmental damage than onshore oil development, this accident stopped all efforts to explore the Coastal Plain for the next six years. It wasn't until House Republicans became the majority party in 1995 that exploring the Coastal Plain was the subject of a policy debate.

To set the stage on this issue, it is important to note that the Arctic National Wildlife Refuge or ANWR is 19.6 million acres. This is the size of the State of South Carolina. Within the refuge is 1.5 million acres that comprise the Coastal Plain. This is about the size of the State of Delaware. Of that total, approximately 92,000 acres are owned by the Kaktovik Inupiat Corporation who was prohibited from developing their own oil and gas resources.

According to the U.S. Fish and Wildlife Service, there are 200 bird species, 46 species of mammals, and 46 species of fish residing within ANWR. None of these species are federally listed as endangered. While it may be our nation's largest refuge, only about 1,000 people visit it each year. It is highly isolated and extremely difficult and expensive to get there.

ANWR is located between oil producing fields to the west at Prudhoe Bay and the Mackensie Delta Region to the east. Prudhoe Bay is 65 miles west of ANWR. Since 1967, this field has produced 12.5 billion barrels of oil and more than 26 trillion cubic feet of gas. It is the largest oil discovery in the history of the United States.

Of the 1.5 million acres of the Coastal Plain, any leasing, exploration, and development would be limited to no more than 2,000 acres. This extraordinarily tiny footprint is the size of Dulles Airport and about one ten thousands of ANWR. By comparison, the Prudhoe Bay field covers 213,543 acres.

After a series of hearings, language authorizing oil and gas exploration and development of the Coastal Plain was incorporated within H.R. 2491, the Balanced Budget Act of 1995. This bill was ultimately approved by both bodies of Congress and submitted to President William J. Clinton. Regrettably, President Clinton exercised his first veto. In a 50-page fact sheet, the Clinton Administration cited 82 reasons for not signing H.R. 2491. Among those reasons was a pledge to never allow the Coastal Plain to be open for energy exploration. Radical environmental organizations continued to misrepresent the region to the American people despite the fact that most of their leadership had never even visited the refuge.

Due to the persistent leadership of Don Young, the House of Representatives voted to authorize energy exploration in the Coastal Plain in 2001, 2003, 2005, 2012, and 2017. On each occasion, Don Young made persuasive arguments. On August 1, 2001 during debate on the Energy Policy Act he said, "I want to remind my colleagues this area 1002 is not ANWR. This area was set-aside in 1980 for oil exploration by Senator Jackson, Congressman Udall, Senator Stevens, and Senator Johnston. It was supposed to be drilled and explored for the American people."

Two years later, Don Young told his colleagues that, "My people the Kaktovik, they want this drilling. The Eskimos that live there want this drilling. They have seen what has happened in Prudhoe Bay, which has in fact increased the population of the caribou, increased the game population overall. We can do this safely."

On February 15, 2012, Don Young implored his colleagues, "Open ANWR. Let's vote on it. Let's provide for this nation. Let's do what's right for the people in this nation. It only covers an area as big as Dulles Airport, less than 3,000 acres will be developed to provide us probably 39 billion barrels of oil, 74 miles away from the pipeline, a pipeline that can deliver 2 million barrels of oil a day to the United States of America, as we have done in the past."

I worked on refuge issues for over 30 years. Other than ANWR and the Izembek National Wildlife Refuge in Alaska, there wasn't a single instance where members who didn't represent either the district or the state injected themselves into a refuge policy debate. These representatives from California, Massachusetts, and New York blatantly violated the Young rule which states that the member who represents the affected Congressional District gets to decide. In this case, it was simply wrong to ignore the wishes of the Alaska Congressional delegation, the Governor of Alaska, the Alaska Legislature, and the people of

Alaska, all who strongly support drilling in the Coastal Plain. Yet, this was exactly what a majority of House Democrats and some Republicans did for 37 years.

The former Chairman of the House Energy and Commerce Committee Billy Tauzin (R-LA) described the ANWR debate best when he said, "I understand somewhat when some members come to the well of this House and say, do not drill in my backyard. Do not explore for energy in the offshore off my state. But I am amazed when members show up on the floor and say, do not do it in someone else's state when they want to do it, areas that were set aside to be productive areas."

With the election of Donald J. Trump as our nation's 45th President on November 6, 2016 the possibility of authorizing exploration within the Coastal Plain became a reality. This would never have occurred in a Hillary Clinton Administration.

At the beginning of the 115th Congress, Don Young introduced H.R. 49, the American Energy Independence and Job Creation Act. Two days later, Alaska's senior Senator Lisa Murkowski proposed S. 49, the Alaska Oil and Gas Production Act. Before any hearings were held on the legislation, Secretary of the Interior Ryan Zinke issued Secretarial Order 3352 on May 31, 2017. This order directed the Assistant Secretaries of Land and Mineral

Management and Water and Science to update the assessment of undiscovered, technically recoverable oil and natural resources in the Section 1002 area. In addition, the order stipulated that, "The 1.5 million acre Coastal Plain of the 19 million acre Arctic National Wildlife Refuge is the largest unexplored, potentially productive geological onshore basin in the United States."

On October 4, 2017, the House debated H. Con. Res. 71, the Budget Resolution for the United States for 2019 through 2027. Incorporated within this legislation was a provision authorizing exploration and development within the Coastal Plain. It had been estimated that this would raise at least $1 billion in new federal revenues.

During consideration of H. Con. Res. 71, Don Young reminded the House that, "It will reduce the debt. Again, I said I expect bids of about $10 billion to $20 billion just to have the right to drill. We will have not only a large amount going into the Treasury, we will have about 776,000 new jobs created by the discovery of this oil."

After disposing of various amendments, the House voted 219 to 206 to approve the legislation. Under Congressional rules only a simple majority was required to approve the annual budget resolution and any reconciliation instructions. In H. Con. Res. 71 both tax reform and ANWR were designated as reconciliation items.

This was extraordinarily important because the U.S. Senate approved H. Con. Res. 71 on October 19, 2017 by a vote of 51 to 49. It is important to remember that reconciliation is not a new procedure. In 2010, the Democrat majority in the House and Senate used the reconciliation process to approve the Health Care and Education Reconciliation Act. This law is now better known as Obama Care.

On November 2, 2017, the Senate Energy and Natural Resources Committee held a hearing on opening the 1002 Area to responsible development. In her opening statement, Chairman Lisa Murkowski noted that, "We meet this morning to consider opening a very small portion of Alaska's 1002 area to responsible energy development, to meet the $1 billion budget reconciliation instruction our Committee received last week. I want to be clear: the 1002 area is not federal wilderness. We should also understand: if we open the 1002 area, the economic benefits will be substantial, our national security will be strengthened, and the environmental impacts will be minimal."

In his testimony, Don Young said, "This is an issue of national security. It is the one weapon Russia is wielding. We could have this security for this nation as a whole. If we are to be energy sufficient to control international incidents we need

ANWR. I hope you have the courage to do what is right for this nation. What is good for Alaska, good for the nation, and good for all the people in the future."

The Committee also heard from Alaska's Lieutenant Governor Byron Mallot who is an Alaskan native and leader of the Tlingit Raven Kwaash Kee Kwaan Clan. He testified that, "Alaska holds development on its North Slope to some of the highest standards in the world, and we have a record of success to show for it. Oil and gas exploration occurs with almost no long-term footprint in Alaska, and areas that are brought into production occupy smaller and smaller spaces with more and more resources accessed. After almost 50 years of activity at Prudhoe Bay – the nation's largest oil field – we can say we have established a record of success we can proudly carry forward."

Finally, the Committee heard from Matthew Rexford the Tribal Administrator of the Native Village of Kaktovik. In his statement, he told the Committee that, "I was raised and live in Kaktovik, Alaska, located inside the 1002 area of ANWR. All the organizations I previously mentioned – Native Village of Kaktovik, Kaktovik Inupiat Corporation, and Voice of the Arctic Inupiat – support oil and gas development there. Attempts to permanently block development in the 1002 – is a slap in the face to our region and its people. It's exactly the same as

239

saying it's okay for everyone else in this country to have a thriving economy, but you can't have one at all. We know development in ANWR can be done safety, because it's already being done safely all over the Arctic."

Two weeks after the hearing, the House considered H.R. 1, the Tax Cuts and Jobs Act. This bill was a bold, pro growth effort to overhaul our outdated Tax Code and unleash the free enterprise system. It accomplished that by reducing taxes by $3.2 trillion. It significantly cut tax rates for businesses and individuals, doubled the standing deduction and child tax credit, and subjected fewer families to the federal estate tax. The House on a vote of 227 to 205 approved it.

On December 20, 2017, the U.S. Senate debate H.R. 1. During its consideration, it approved a provision sponsored by Alaska Senators Lisa Murkowski and Dan Sullivan directing the Secretary of Interior to establish a competitive oil and gas program in the non-wilderness portion of the Coastal Plain. Specifically, it required the Secretary to conduct at least two area-wide lease sales within the next ten years. The first lease sale must occur no later than December 22, 2021. In addition, the Secretary was directed to issue any necessary rights-of-way or easements across the Coastal Plain for the exploration, development, production or transportation of oil and gas resources. It also limited these activities to no more than 2,000 surface acres of the Coastal Plain and the language stipulated that any revenues derived from these lease sales will be split equally between the State of Alaska and the federal government. The U.S. Senate voted 51 to 49 in favor of H.R. 1.

After members of the House and Senate Conference Committee, which included Don Young, completed their negotiations, the Senate approved the Conference Report on December 20, 2017 by a vote of 51 to 48. Incorporated within the final bill was the Murkowski and Sullivan provision opening the Coastal Plain. Later that day, the House voted 224 to 201. During debate in the People's House, Speaker Paul Ryan (R-WI) said, "Some people have been working here since I was in the second grade on this project" as he pointed at Don Young. He went on to say, "After decades and decades in this chamber, we are opening up a small non-wilderness area of the Alaska National Wildlife Refuge for responsible development. This is the most ambitious step we have taken in years to secure our energy future."

For the first time in 22 years, both the House and Senate voted to allow long overdue exploration in the Coastal Plain. Unlike 1995, however, President Donald Trump signed this historic legislation into law on December 22, 2017. In his signing statement, the President noted that, "This is the biggest tax cuts and reform in the history of our country. In addition, we have ANWR – we're opening up ANWR for drilling. They've tried to get that for 40 years. They're tried to get that even during the Reagan Administration. They could never get it. That alone would be a big bill if that even happened, but that's even part of this."

During the past 40 years, Alaska has had six U.S. Senators: Ted Stevens, Mike Gravel, Frank Murkowski, Lisa Murkowski, Mark Begich, and Dan Sullivan. It has had one representative in the House of Representatives and his name is Don Young. No one has ever worked longer or harder to get a specific piece of legislation signed into law. Along with the Alaskan Pipeline Act, the National Wildlife Refuge System Improvement Act, and SAFETEA-LU, this huge landmark achievement is a tribute to his dedication, persistence, and commitment to the people of Alaska.

While no one can accurately predict how many billions of barrels of oil and trillions of cubic feet will be extracted from the Coastal Plain, how many tens of thousands of jobs will be created, and how many billions will be deposited in the U.S. Treasury, none of this would have occurred without the leadership of Don Young. He simply refused to give up, he out served many of the loudest opponents of oil and gas exploration in the Coastal Plain, and he ignored the millions of dollars that environmental groups spent to misrepresent this issue. With the help of Senators Lisa Murkowski and Dan Sullivan the stars were finally aligned to move this legislation to the finish line.

In his own words, Don Young told his Alaskan constituents, "I am proud to support this measure and what it means for Alaskan families and businesses. This bill marks the 13th time the House has voted to allow for responsible resource development in the 1002 area of the Arctic National Wildlife Refuge, which is crucial to the future of the American energy sector. Opening ANWR means jobs for Alaskans, economic growth and securing America's energy independence for generations to come. I have fought this battle for over 40 years." On December 22, 2017, Don Young won the battle for thousands of new jobs, billions to the U.S. Treasury, and a giant step towards energy independence for the United States of America!

CHAPTER 10: FINAL REFLECTIONS

Since his first election in 1964, Don Young has won 27 General Elections. He lost only once in the 1972 Congressional Race against Congressman Nick Begich. Sadly, the Congressman's plane disappeared on its way to Juneau and in December 1972 he was declared legally dead. Don Young has defeated the President of the Alaska Federation of Natives, Alaskan State Senators, Alaskan House Representatives, Mayors, a future Governor of Alaska, and Nick Begich's widow. His largest winning percentage was in 2002 when he defeated Democrat Clifford Mark Greene by 130,000 votes. His closest re-election occurred in 1992 when he beat the Mayor of Valdez, John S. Devins by 947 votes. This is a remarkable record of political success.

Don Young has served with nine different Democrat and Republican Presidents. These were Richard Nixon, Gerald R. Ford, Jimmy Carter, Ronald W. Reagan, George H. Bush, William J. Clinton, George W. Bush, Barack Obama, and Donald J. Trump. While in the House of Representatives, he served with nine different Speakers of the House including Carl Albert, Thomas P. O'Neill, Jim Wright, Thomas Foley, Newt Gingrich, John Hastert, Nancy Pelosi, John Boehner, and Paul Ryan.

Since becoming a Member of Congress, Don Young has sponsored 1,017 bills. Of this total, 143 pieces of his legislation have been signed into law. This includes 81 bills Don Young introduced as the lead sponsor and 62 Don Young sponsored bills that were incorporated within another House or Senate bill and signed into law. Among the list of his key legislative accomplishments are: Alaskan Pipeline Act of 1973, Fishery Conservation and Management Act of 1976, Sustainable Fisheries Act of 1996, National Wildlife Refuge System Improvement Act of 1997, SAFETEA-LU Act of 2005, and the American Energy Independence and Job Creation Act of 2017 (ANWR).

While most Americans never refer to a federal law by its House or Senate number, H.R. 39 is a number that is well known to the citizens of Alaska. This is because in 1980, Morris Udall introduced H.R. 39 as the infamous Alaska National Interest Lands Conservation Act. Upon becoming the Chairman of the House Resources Committee in 1995, Don Young choose this number to reauthorize the Magnuson-Stevens Fishery Conservation and Management Act. Over the past 23 years, Don Young has used H.R. 39 on eight different occasions and two of those bills were signed into law.

As of June 1, 2018, which was his 16,515[th] day in the House of Representatives, Don Young had casted 24,491 votes. What this means is that his voting percentage was 85 percent of the 28,781 substantive and procedural votes

246

that took place over this period of public service.

In terms of personal relationships, Don Young has frequently said he has no enemies in the House of Representatives. In fact, he has had a number of close personal friends. These include Bill Brewster (D-OK), John Dingell (D-MI), Jack Fields (R-TX), Duncan Hunter (R-CA), Jim Oberstar (D-MN), and Gerry Studds. In the current Congress, the list includes Congressmen Ken Calvert (R-CA), Jim Costa (D-CA), Brian Mast (R-FL), Colin Peterson (D-MN), and Steve Russell (R-OK).

On August 11, 1989, one of those friends, the late Congressman from Massachusetts, Gerry Studds told a hearing audience in Anchorage Alaska that, "We are here at the invitation of the Ranking Member of the Subcommittee, Representative Don Young, who has played a major role not only in the passage of the Magnuson Act but in virtually every other major piece of fisheries – related legislation of the last two decades. It is my pleasure to introduce one of the great defenders of fisheries and coastlines, Representative Don Young.

Don Young also had an extremely close relationship with Alaska's Senior Senator, Ted Stevens. Sadly, Ted Stevens died in a tragic plane crash in Dillingham, Alaska on August 9, 2010. Upon hearing the terrible news, Don Young said, "Ted was a very close, personal friend of me and my family. I used to babysit his kids, and he would babysit mine. He's been my mentor, first in the state legislature, and then as our Senior Senator and I will miss him a great deal."

His closest relationship was with his beloved wife of 46 years, Lu Fredson. She was his advisor, confident, friend, protector, mother to their two daughters, and grandmother to 14 beautiful children. I will always remember a trip that John Rayfield and I made in June 1996 to Toms River, New Jersey with Lu Young. We were going to visit the Edwin Forsythe National Wildlife Refuge and Lu Young was going to join her husband for the wedding of Young staffer Jessica Scallon. As we met in the House Rayburn Building garage, Don Young instructed us to drive carefully, not to exceed the speed limit, and to protect his dear wife. However, long before we completed our 192 mile journey, Lu Young looked at John and said something to the effect that, "John, you are driving too slowly. Get up the road. My kids call me Lead Foot Lu." Ironically, Don Young named one of our nation's most important highway bills for Lu. Sadly, she passed away on August 2, 2009.

While not expecting to re-marry, on his birthday June 9, 2015, Don Young wed Anne Garland Walton in the U.S. Capitol. The House Chaplain Father Patrick Conroy officiated the marriage and it was witnessed by then Speaker of the House,

John Boehner. After the ceremony, Don Young said, "We have both known great love and experienced deep heartbreak. In many ways neither of us even thought we would find love again, but sometimes life surprises you."

I first met the Congressman for All of Alaska in March 1985 upon my appointment to the Merchant Marine and Fisheries Subcommittee on Panama Canal and Outer Continental Shelf. Under the Committee rules, each Subcommittee Ranking Member was permitted to select a Professional Staffer to represent them. These positions were known as Clause 5's.

Upon becoming the Ranking Republican of the Panama Canal Subcommittee, Jack Fields of Humble, Texas was allowed to choose a Clause 5. He selected me. It didn't take me long to recognize that Don Young of Alaska was a committed, dedicated, persistent, and tireless advocate for the people of Alaska. He views his job quite literally as their representative charged with the solemn responsibility of improving their lives, their livelihoods, and their future. Don Young has spent more than 50 years effectively representing Alaskans at the local, state, and federal levels.

In 1993, Don Young became the Ranking Republican member of the House Natural Resources Committee. This committee was of vital importance to the State of Alaska. At the same time, Jack

Fields became the Ranking Republican member of the Merchant Marine and Fisheries Committee. He appointed me as his Chief-of-Staff. Just two years later, Don Young was the new Chairman of the Resources Committee and the Merchant Marine Committee was abolished.

After the election, Don Young visited my office to inquire about my future employment and those of the other Republican staff who had lost their jobs. Without hesitation, I told him that it was my fondest hope that I could work for him in the 104th Congress. Fortunately, he agreed and this was the kickoff of the most challenging, exciting, and rewarding 20 years of my professional career. I can never thank him enough for his confidence.

On January 11, 1995, the Natural Resources Committee met to organize for the 104th Congress. During this meeting, the Committee was scheduled to vote to approve the Committee rules, the Legislative and Oversight Plan for the next two years, and to hire Committee staff. After 22 long years as a member of the minority, Don Young was anxious to have these items quickly debated and approved. However, during the middle of those deliberations, he was handed a note from his wife, Lu who was sitting in the front row of the Committee Room. According to my colleague Lisa Pittman, who was Deputy Chief Counsel at that time and sitting on the dais next to the Chairman, it simply said: "Smile More."

While I loved my job, it was nearly short circuited during the first six months as Staff Director of the Subcommittee on Fisheries, Wildlife, and Oceans, when my Subcommittee Chairman Jim Saxton decided to hold a hearing on H.R. 353, the Black Bear Protection Act. John Edward Porter, a moderate Republican, who frequently supported animal rights legislation introduced this bill. In this case, his bill prohibited the export of American black bear viscera. In Asia, there were farms with thousands of captive black bears whose bile was extracted for Traditional Chinese Medicine.

Although Jim Saxton was a life long bear hunter, he wanted to be helpful to his colleagues Sherwood Boehlert (R-NY), Connie Morella (R-MD), Porter Goss (R-FL), Chris Shays (R-CT), and Chris Smith (R-NJ) who were co-sponsors of the bill. By so doing, he put me in a difficult position because I would be responsible for scheduling the hearing and selecting most of the witnesses. However, before issuing a single invitation, Don Young called me to ask if such a hearing was being planned.

He reminded me that bear hunting was a proud tradition, especially in Alaska, black bear populations were thriving in the United States, and I could hold this hearing but it would likely be my last. I got the message loud and clear.

251

There was no hearing on H.R. 353, the Black Bear Protection Act.

Upon becoming Chairman, one of Don Young's pet peeves was the use of cell phones. It was common in the early 1990's for member phones to ring often and loudly during Committee meetings. Don Young's reaction, shared by many, was that these disruptions were rude to the audience, Committee members, and the witnesses. In the writing of the new Committee rules, it was, therefore, not surprising, that they would include, "The use of cellular telephones is prohibited on the Committee dais or in the Committee hearing rooms during a meeting or hearing in the Committee."

While this largely solved the problem, there were members who forgot or decided not to mute their phones. In almost every case, the Chairman would look sternly at the offending party and the member would leave the dais or the Committee. However, I vividly remember the day the Full Committee was holding an important hearing on energy development in this country. Suddenly, a loud ringing sound filled the Committee, the Chairman searched for the perpetrator, and then he simply smiled because sitting in the front row holding her cell phone was Senator Mary Landrieu of Louisiana. Mary Landrieu was a charming and charismatic Senator well liked by members of both political parties.

On September 10, 1993, President William J. Clinton made history by naming Mollie Beattie, the Vermont Commissioner of Forests, Parks, and Recreation as the first female Director of the U.S. Fish and Wildlife Service. Mollie Beattie, who has the 11th Director, testified before my Subcommittee on Fisheries, Wildlife, and Oceans on three separate occasions in 1995.

The first time occurred on February 16, 1995, when she defended the agency's funding request for Fiscal Year 1996. During her testimony, she discussed endangered species, fish hatcheries, marine mammals, subsistence hunting, and wildlife refuges. When talking about native Alaskans, Don Young emphasized the importance of handicraft products by introducing an "oosik." I suspect this was the first --- if not only --- time an oosik was used as a prop at a Congressional hearing.

This walrus bone is used to construct knife handles. Together with crafts made of scrimshaw, these products generate important tourist dollars for Alaskan natives.

Sadly, Mollie Beattie passed away of cancer on June 5, 1996. In recognition of her valuable service to this nation, Don Young introduced H.R. 3706, the Mollie Beattie Wilderness Act. This measure permanently designated for her the 8 million acres of wilderness contained within the Arctic National Wildlife Refuge.

After shepherding the measure through the legislative process, President William J. Clinton signed Don Young's bill into law on July 29, 1996."

In the 110th Congress, the Democrats had a majority in both Houses of Congress and Don Young was elected to serve as the Ranking Republican on the House Natural Resources Committee. On April 24, 2008, Paul Jenkins of the Anchorage Times wrote, "For 35 years, he has been a staple of Alaska politics, an experienced and integral partner of an incredibly effective Congressional delegation. He is a big part of Alaska's history since statehood."

In late October 2008, my wife Gayle and I traveled to Alaska to volunteer for Don Young's re-election. During that cycle, Don Young was engaged in a difficult race with now Anchorage Mayor Ethan Berkowitz. In fact, Dr. Stuart Rothenberg a Political Science Professor at Bucknell University and author of the Rothenberg Political Report predicted that Don Young was the House Republican most likely to lose on November 4, 2008. He was wrong and later admitted that, "My single biggest rating mistake was rating Republican Rep. Don Young of Alaska's at-large House seat as "Democrat Favored."

We spent nearly ten days waving signs for Don Young along Northern Lights Boulevard in the freezing cold and delivering campaign material to homes throughout Anchorage. We were joined in this effort by Mike Anderson, Holly Craft, Pam Day, Erik Elam, Steve Hansen, Meredith Kenny, Paul Milotte, Chad Padgett, Dave Whaley, and C. J. Zane. When the ballots were counted, Don Young won the election by 16,379 votes. We celebrated his stunning victory at the Egan Civil and Convention Center. The atmosphere was electric and humbling because the people of Alaska had spoken.

On January 10, 2018, Don Young was honored for becoming the 48th Dean of the House of Representatives. He was the first Republican to hold this title since Gilbert N. Haugen of Iowa in 1933. In his remarks, Speaker of the House Paul Ryan said, "This milestone is not just a matter of longevity, but the word that comes to mind when you think of Don Young is "loyalty." This man is fiercely loyal to Alaska. He fights hard for what he believes is right. Just look at ANWR. Don Young has been working on ANWR for 45 years. When we passed H.R. 1 in the House that was the 13th time he passed an ANWR bill, and it finally made it into law. Don Young is a man of this institution. He believes in the work that we do. I thank Don Young for his service to Alaska and to this country."

Democrat Leader Nancy Pelosi added her voice to the ceremony, when she said, "Despite our differences, it is clear that Don cares deeply about our Nation. Don serves because, in his words, he is 'enthusiastic about meeting people and trying to solve their problems.' The motto of the State of Alaska is 'North to the future.' In his commitment to progress and better futures for the people of Alaska, Don honors those words."

Finally, the new Dean of the House told his colleagues that, "My greatest honor has been being able to achieve results for my State. I am the only Congressman from the whole State of Alaska and I love it. I believe in bipartisanship. I believe in this body to lead this Nation. Nine Presidents, the House has its job to do regardless of who the President is. I thank my wife, who is in the audience up there in the gallery. A man gets lucky usually once in his life. I got lucky twice. I want to thank my colleagues. Being the dean will not change me. I will still holler "Vote." I will sometimes get out of line. But in doing so, remember, it comes from my heart and my heart is in this House."

In 1980, Jack Fields of Humble, Texas decided to challenge seven-term Democrat incumbent Bob Eckhardt. As a first time candidate, he ran a brilliant campaign. For nearly two years, he knocked on thousands of doors in Texas' 8th Congressional District and he shared his vision of government to his future constituents. On Election Day, November 4, 1980, he defeated Bob Eckhardt by 4,900 votes. He became the first Republican ever elected to this District and he ran ahead of Ronald Reagan who became our nation's

40th President. In the House of Representatives he served 14 years with the Congressman for All of Alaska on the House Merchant Marine and Fisheries Committee.

Reflections of Congressman Jack Fields

I first met Don Young in early 1981 when the House Merchant Marine and Fisheries Committee held its organizational meeting for the 97th Congress. When I arrived, Don Young was already a senior member of the Committee with a long list of legislative accomplishments. He was widely viewed by his Committee colleagues as a colorful, effective, and tireless advocate for his Alaskan constituents.

We bonded over our mutual love of hunting and the importance of wildlife conservation. Both of us had traveled to southern Africa. We had witnessed the beauty and destruction of Africa's iconic species of elephants, lions, and rhinoceros. We understood that unless these animals have an economic value they would be killed for food, for the protection of the local villagers, and for profit.

In 1979, there were 1.3 million elephants living in the wild in Africa. In less than a decade, there were fewer than 400,000. They were being indiscriminately slaughtered by roving bands of heavily armed poachers who were killing them for their ivory. As a result of this senseless tragedy, Don Young and I sought a legislative solution.

As a result of Congressional hearings and meetings with dozens of animal rights, conservation, environmental, and hunting organizations, our solution was incorporated within Title II of the Endangered Species Act Amendments of 1988. Specifically, our language established the African Elephant Conservation Fund, created a moratorium and prohibitions on the export and import of certain raw and worked ivory, and allowed individuals to import sport-hunted elephant trophies legally taken in an ivory producing country that had submitted an ivory quota. This provision was critical to ensuring that local villagers would protect the wild elephants living in their communities.

In 1994, Don Young and I worked with the Chairman of the Merchant Marine and Fisheries Committee, Gerry Studds, to craft language to the Marine Mammal Protection Act of 1994. In this case, we were trying to help conserve polar bears in Alaska, Canada, and Russia. There were growing populations of polar bears in certain Canadian provinces and American hunters were prohibited from bringing a polar bear trophy back into the United States.

This made little conservation sense. Hunters, except Americans, throughout the world, were legally taking old bull polar bears in Canada. Our citizens wanted an opportunity to hunt these magnificent animals and to contribute through their expenditure of thousands of dollars in fees to the overall conservation of the species. Our solution that was incorporated within Public Law 103-238 directed the Secretary of the Interior to issue permits for the importation of a polar bear trophy from those applicants who had the necessary documentation to prove that a polar bear was legally taken in Canada. In addition, Canada was required to have a monitored hunting program, scientifically sound quotas, and these hunts could not contribute to the illegal trade in bear parts.

Those who harvested a polar bear in Canada were required to pay $1,000 for a trophy import permit. All of this money was used for polar bear conservation programs in Alaska and Russia.

Since my retirement from Congress in 1997, I have continued to work closely with the Congressman from All of Alaska. In fact, it has been Don Young who has successfully extended the

259

African Elephant Conservation Fund and the Rhinoceros and Tiger Conservation Fund through his sponsorship of the necessary legislation. Without these funds, these iconic species would have continued their slide toward extinction. Because of them, our children and grandchildren will be able to see wild African elephants, rhinoceros, and tigers. This speaks volumes about our nation's commitment to wildlife conservation and the effective leadership of the Congressman from Fort Yukon, Alaska.

During the current Congress, I am strongly supporting Don Young's African Elephant Conservation and Legal Ivory Possession Act. This important legislation would direct the placement of a Fish and Wildlife Service Law Enforcement Officer in each African range country; it addresses the treatment of legally imported elephant ivory; clarifies sport-hunted elephant trophies; and extends the vital African Elephant Conservation Fund.

Over the past 30 years, it has been a great pleasure working with Don Young. From my vantage point, he is an almost irreplaceable part of the House of Representatives. He is a problem solver. But let there be no doubt of his intense passion to improve the lives of all Alaskans. I am proud to call him a colleague and more importantly a friend.

Don Young has always believed that you can accomplish great achievements in the legislative process if you are willing to work in a bipartisan manner. One of his best partners and friends in those efforts was the gentleman from Ardmore, Oklahoma, Congressman Bill Brewster who was a member of the Democrat Party.

As lifelong conservationists, these two members fought to improve the Migratory Bird Treaty Act of 1918 and the National Wildlife Refuge System. In addition, Bill Brewster introduced the Sportsmen's Bill of Rights Bill to ensure that federal lands were open for hunting and fishing.

Bill Brewster was an outstanding representative of Oklahoma's 3rd Congressional District. While now retired from the Congress, Bill Brewster continues his important wildlife conservation work as an active member of the Shikar Safari Club. As a nation, we need more legislators, like Bill Brewster, who are willing to sit down, regardless of political party, and work constructively for the good of the American people.

Reflections of Congressman Bill Brewster

On November 7, 1990, I had the great honor to be elected a member of Congress to represent Oklahoma's 3ʳᵈ Congressional District. This district affectionately known as "Little Dixie" was comprised of 21 counties and 524,000 hard working, God fearing, and patriotic Americans. It was the second largest district in the state, the birthplace of Speaker Carl Albert, and it included my hometown of Ardmore, Oklahoma.

Upon being sworn-into office, it did not take me long to establish a lifelong friendship with the Congressman from Fort Yukon, Don Young. We had many common interests and despite being members of different political parties, we were interested in solving problems facing the American people. Among those key problems was energy independence. After experiencing boycotts, gas lines, and disruptions in our economy by certain Middle Eastern countries, Don and I were committed to increasing U.S. oil and gas production.

My home state of Oklahoma is a major energy producer in this country. In 2014, we produced 128 million barrels of oil and the world's largest oil storage facility is located in the 3ʳᵈ Congressional District in Cushing. Throughout my Congressional career, I sponsored and co-sponsored dozens of pieces of legislation to increase our oil and gas resources. One of those measures was Don Young's legislation to open a small portion of the Coastal Plain of the Arctic National Wildlife Refuge to responsible exploration, development, and production. I was pleased to join in this fight. I knew Don Young would never give up and I could not have been happier when President Donald Trump signed the Young Coastal Plain bill into law.

Like Alaska, the 3rd Congressional District has units of the National Wildlife Refuge System. There were hundreds of my constituents who visited the Little River National Wildlife Refuge and the Tishomingo National Wildlife Refuge to hunt and fish. These sportsmen and sportswomen understood that these federal lands had been paid for with their tax dollars and excise fees. They strongly felt, as I did, that wildlife dependent recreation must be a priority use within the refuge system.

For these reasons, I was pleased to join with Don in sponsoring the National Wildlife Refuge System Improvement Act. Don was committed to allowing sportsmen and sportswomen access to these federal lands and to ensure that wildlife dependent users such as hunting, fishing, wildlife observation, photography, environmental education and interpretation were priority activities within the refuge system. After working in a bipartisan manner with the Clinton Administration, Don Young's bill passed the Congress with only one dissenting vote and President William J. Clinton signed it into law. This was a remarkable legislative achievement and one that will be enjoyed by hunters and fishermen throughout this country for many years in the future.

It is also ironic that Don and I sponsored the National Parks and National Wildlife Refuge Systems Freedom Act. Under this bill, state employees would have been permitted to work at a national park or wildlife refuge during a showdown of the federal government. Sadly, this bill was not enacted into law, which is too bad because this authority would have been helpful during the most recent government shutdown.

Finally, any discussion of my dear friend Don Young would be incomplete without highlighting his commitment to wildlife conservation. No one in the Congress has worked harder for sound conservation principles both here in the United States and abroad than Don Young. For the past two decades, he has led the fight to save imperiled populations of African and Asian elephants, rhinoceros, and tigers. It is not an exaggeration to suggest that without his leadership these iconic species would be on the brink of extinction.

As a member of the conservation organization, Shikar Safari Club International, I have watched him work tirelessly to ensure that in the case of African elephants these animals continue to have an economic value. In the United States, we all love elephants. They are truly majestic creatures but we don't live with them like the African villagers I have visited. Unless you have sport hunters who are willing to spend thousands of American dollars in Africa, there is no motivation for a local villager to protect a 13,000-pound bull elephant who is a real danger to his families' existence. The money spent by hunters is directly invested in local clinics, hospitals, and schools. None of this would occur without conservation champions like my friend Don Young.

I am proud to have called Don Young my dear friend for nearly 30 years. I have the highest trust in his leadership. In fact, this trust extended to my suggestion that he hire my former Chief of Staff and 3rd District constituent, Colin Chapman. Colin became one of the best Chiefs of Staff for Don Young and he continues to make everyone in Oklahoma proud of his work.

I am pleased to offer these reflections and I am confident that the new Dean

265

of the House will continue to be an effective advocate and leader for the people of Alaska. We need more Congressmen like Don Young who are willing to work together with members of both political parties to solve our nation's problems. There is nothing wrong with bipartisanship. Don Young and I proved that during our joint service in the Congress.

During the 1973 Special Election to fill the seat vacated by Congressman Nick Begich, the Republican National Committee decided to invest money and volunteers to elect Don Young. One of those volunteers was James "Jim" Lexo. After winning the election, Jim was hired by the new Congressman for All of Alaska to serve on his first Congressional staff. During the next two decades, Jim did a superb job as Chief of Staff, Executive Assistance and Legislative Director.

As most seasoned politicians will tell you the first re-election campaign is usually the most difficult. Jim Lexo was certainly up to this challenge and he provided Don Young with invaluable advice, guidance, loyalty, and support. While hundreds of people worked for Don Young over the past 45 years, Jim was one of the first hires and one of the most talented.

Reflections of James Lexo

I first met Don Young shortly after New Year's Day in 1973. I was working at the Republican National Committee and we had finished the 1972 Presidential race two months earlier. My new plan was to get a job on Capitol Hill with a Congressman. I did interview at the White House with Patrick Buchanan who was in charge of the President's daily briefing at the time. I declined after he told me it was an 80 hours a week job for a $10K annual salary.

Then one day my boss asked me if I would like to go to Alaska to help a "riverboat captain" win the Congressional seat. I suspect he asked me because I grew up in Buffalo and knew how to handle the cold. I landed in Anchorage where the high temperature averaged maybe 10 degrees. Walter Hickel was supporting the campaign so they put me up at the Cook (Hotel), which at that time had one tower.

In the 1972 general election, I worked for Jack Kemp on his campaign to win the Congressional seat in the Buffalo area. Jack was very articulate and polished. I could listen to the same speech ten times a day and not get bored. I think it was the day after I landed that Don was scheduled to speak at the Anchorage Chamber of

Commerce. The luncheon was at the Sheffield Hotel (since changed) and I remember standing in the back of a packed room.

Don got up to speak and I thought...Holy Crap, we have our work cut out for us. As he is known to do he murdered the Queen's English and was rough "as a cob." Not what I was used to. Over time, I would learn that this is what a lot of people like about Don. He has no pretentions and "what you see is what you get"...pretty refreshing in the political arena.

Don told me about his background. How his parents told him they could not afford to keep him on the farm after he returned home from the Army. Don said his dad read him Call of the Wild as a kid and it always stuck with him. So he caught a steamer to Alaska to seek fame and fortune. In his early Alaska years he worked construction; in the logging industry; in the fishing industry; and most anything else that paid a decent buck. Out of work one winter, someone said, "Hey, you have a teaching degree. There is an opening in Fort Yukon. You should apply." He did and that is how he came to make Ft. Yukon his home.

Don was told the salary he would make and that he would get accommodations and other benefits. He got the salary and that was about it. For accommodations they put him with a married couple in what was probably a 500 square foot home. After weeks on the sofa, Don found his own accommodations. He met his first wife Lu when he went to the local movie house. She was serving popcorn. Lu's family was the Fredson, a fairly well known family in the area. Her father was apparently the first college educated native in the region.

Don and Lu used to tell a cute story on why he ran for Congress. Don was in the State Senate and they were both in Juneau during a long session. Both said they were miserable and wanted to go back to Ft. Yukon permanently. Then Don said we can't be quitters though supposedly, Lu said, "Well let's run for Congress. We will lose...then we can move home." Don did lose, but the problem is he lost to a man everyone knew was dead and gone. It took an extra month to declare Begich officially dead and to call for a special election

My job at the RNC was opposition research. So that was one duty I took on. I also ended up helping Malcolm Roberts with the advertising themes and content. Don's opponent was Emil Notti, a native Alaskan from the North Slope. Emil had been Chair of the Democratic Party at the time. The politics surrounding Alaskan natives was heavy given the Alaska Native Claims Settlement Act had only passed two years earlier. This was an important step in clearing the way for the Alaska oil pipeline authorization. Don's slogan was and still is "Congressman for all Alaska". Some Democrats tried to claim it was racially motivated, implying that Notti would only represent the native Alaskans. This was brought up at an AFN meeting during the election and Don let them "have it" as he is known to do. His primary point was that he was married to a native Alaskan, he taught school in a native village, and he represented mostly Alaska natives during tenure in the Juneau legislature.

The National Republican Congressional Committee sent several people to work the campaign. The top guy was Ed Terrill and with him came MaryAnn Miller. Ed was the guy with the campaign management experience and MaryAnn was the one with grassroots, get out the vote experience. The first campaign headquarters was on Fifth Avenue and donated by the owner of the Ford dealership. The location was free but not ideal. On one side of the HQ was a strip joint and the other side was a gay bar. Don likes to tell the story how the first day on the job, Ed Terrill asked Don where to go for lunch. Don directed him next door to the strip bar. Ed came back...after some time however...to protest on how Don duped him into going to the strip bar. The next day Ed again asked Don where to go to lunch and of course, Don sent him to the other side of the HQ. Ed didn't stay long and came back realizing he had fallen into the same trap again.

It was a very tight race and toward the end of the campaign I found a quote by Emil Notti that certainly looked to be soft on gun control. In Alaska, especially back then; this could be a deathblow. We distributed leaflets and spread the word. Some say it might have been the difference between winning and losing.

MaryAnn Miller's grass roots effort included phone banks to turn out the voters. All the unoccupied rooms in the Captain Cook were used to make calls. In a special election, it all about getting your voters to the polls since there are no other races to attract the voters. Don ended up winning by one percent. At the election eve event when it became clear that Don would be elected, I recall him turning to me and saying, "you are the only person I know in DC...I want you to work for me." It was sort of like the movie "The Candidate" where Robert Redford wins a Senate seat in California and then turns to his aide and says, "What do we do now?" The job offer was exactly what I was hoping for. I would be working for a Congressman and I would not have to start as a file clerk.

So we get back to D.C. and go into what was Nick Begich's office. In the office there was one secretary and one dictionary. That was it. Not a shred of paper; no case files to follow up on...nothing. Apparently, Begich's Administrative Aide took the election in a bad way and ordered that everything had to go. It turned out that Guy Martin, Begich's chief legislative aide, was helpful. He met with us and said the secretary's name is Edith Vivian and she would like to stay on with us if we will have her. He explained what else had gone on in the office and said if he could be of further help to let him know.

One joke in Congress is that it takes you a week to find the bathroom. So when Don needed one he would head down the Longworth halls in search of relief. Finally, Edith Vivian...who we did hire...said, "Congressman, you have a bathroom right off of your office." To say we got off to a slow start is a great understatement. Neither Don nor I knew what the heck we were supposed to do. To help out, the NRCC sent over Max Rohm to be Chief Administrator. Max was about 78 and he brought two young ladies with him...both around 75. One was a raging alcoholic. Don said Max was good at opening doors for him, but that was about it. Max did not last long. Neither did his friends.

272

We managed to staff up just in time for the Alaskan Pipeline Authorization to hit Congress. An energy crisis plus a sympathetic President Nixon and Vice President Ford helped make the pipeline a reality. In between time working the pipeline bill and learning the other duties of the office, Don started flying back to Alaska nearly every weekend. First term Congressmen are the most vulnerable in the next election and one thing about Don, he never takes an election for granted. The House is off Friday and Monday, and when Alaska is your district, you need both those days just to fly. That left Saturday and Sunday to hit the rubber chicken circuit. Don developed a nasty rash on one hand and he asked the Doctor what was wrong. The Doc said, "your body is somewhere between here and Alaska. So it is messing with you."

After the office got staffed and we got the pipeline passed and we got through the impeachment of Nixon, things started to settle down. The next big legislative effort was the 200-mile fishing limit. Don was truly a leader in this effort. He decided the U.S. needed to take unilateral action because the U.N. would never find terms agreeable to all nations. Don co-sponsored legislation with Rep. Gerry Studds of Massachusetts. Studds represented a lot of the fishermen who lived off catching fish in the Grand Banks in the North Atlantic. So the bill infamously became

273

*known as the "Young Studds" bill.
How could you be against that?*

*The years following the passage of the
200-mile fishing limit saw record
numbers of fish and crab caught in
Alaska. Fishermen from Ketchikan to
Adak (especially Kodiak) became big
Don Young fans. During the Carter
years we were on the defensive fighting
Carter's efforts to "lock up" Alaska's
resources in a federal land grab. The
Alaska National Interest Lands
Conservation Act – ANILCA- became a
huge battle between Carter and the
environmentalists versus Alaska
interests. Alaskans saw it as the feds
putting Alaska's resources off limits.*

*Another controversial bill promoted by
the Friends of the Animals was the
banning of the "leg hold trap." This is
the common device used in trapping
animals for their fur. Don did trapping
among his many other endeavors
around Ft. Yukon and he sat on the
House Interior Committee where the
legislation was under consideration.
Cleveland Amory was the primary
proponent and he brought America's
sweetheart Mary Tyler Moore to testify.
As she started to testify Don started
grilling her in a very unfriendly way,
basically trying to determine if she
knew anything about trapping. His
aggressive questioning actually brought
Mary Tyler Moore to tears, which
ended up being in a bunch of tabloids.*

We never had such hate mail as we did from that incident.

During the hearing Don also produced a leg hold trap...probably mink size...to demonstrate it is not that violent. He set the trap and then stuck his hand in it. I am sure it hurt a bit, but it did not break the skin or take a finger off. Some fellow in the back of the room immediately stood up holding a bear trap and said, "Here Congressman, put your hand in this one!" Don was quick...he said that particular trap was illegal and suggested the fellow should be arrested unless the trap had been welded shut.

Throughout this we are running every two years, which meant we were always campaigning and always raising money. And it seemed the elections did not get a lot easier. We had a number of close elections, but we always came through. Don would send me to Alaska around June or July of each election year to manage the campaign and I was allowed to come back in November...if we won. I figured that if I wanted to keep my job, I better do all I can to get him re-elected.

In one of the early campaigns we were going around Anchorage to speaking engagements. At the end of the day, Dick Shepherd, our District Manager said let's go get a beer. Dick was a bit of a crazy guy when it came to the social

275

life. He drove us to one of the many strip joints that popped up during the building of the pipeline. Don said, "I can't go in there." Dick said sure you can, just pull your hat down a bit. We went in and sat and people started saying "Hi Don". He had forgotten to take off a big name tag made of ivory that was pinned on his jacket. One group worked for the BLM. Art Kennedy was in that group. We knew they would not say anything because they had the same concern about it getting out in the public.

In another campaign we landed in Fairbanks and immediately got into a small plane flown by Paul Haggland. In Fairbanks I grabbed the gray Samsonite suitcase of Don's and gave it to our Fairbanks rep, Ellen. Unfortunately, there were a lot of gray Samsonite suitcases back then. At the end of the day was a formal event raising money for a charity. I get Don back to the Travelers Hotel and I go to the coffee shop for a breather. Next, I get paged and it is Don saying, "Get up here and get this suitcase. It is full panties...and they don't fit." I ran back out to the airport and I will be damned if his suitcase was not still going around in circles on the belt. I replaced it with the other gray Samsonite and got back in the hotel.

Some of the best stories I ever heard was when Don would get with some of the

old gang he served with in Juneau.
They were Clem Tillion, Jay Hammond,
Jack Coghill, Jay Kertula, Ted Stevens
and others. Their stories about the early
statehood days were unbelievable. They
did some really crazy stuff. One story is
that apparently, Ted Stevens, who was
a force of nature, would always take a
big gulp of water before starting one of
his long dissertations. One of the
Senators substituted vodka for the
water one day and they all delighted to
see Ted Stevens turn all sorts of colors
when he gulped it down.

After proudly serving this nation in
the United States Marine Corps and
graduating from the University of Alaska
Fairbanks, Rod Moore was hired by Don
Young on January 1, 1977. During the next
18 years, he served with distinction as a
Legislative Assistant in his personal office
and his Counsel on the House Merchant
Marine and Fisheries Committee.

I had the privilege of working with
Rod on that Committee from March 1985
to January 1995. During that time, I always
valued our friendship and respected Rod
as a true professional who Don Young
could always depend upon to get the job
done. Unlike many House Committees, the
Merchant Marine and Fisheries Committee
was not highly partisan. While there were
differences on policy issues, these were
more likely the result of regional concerns
and not party affiliation. As a result, Rod,

Moore, who was a highly effective spokesman for Don Young, was able to form alliances with Democrat staff of Committee members John Breaux(D-LA), Walter Jones (D-NC), and Gerry Studds (D-MA).

On the Merchant Marine and Fisheries Committee, Rod Moore had a large portfolio of issues. These included the Arctic National Wildlife Refuge, Marine Mammal Protection Act, Merchant Marine Act, Oil Pollution Act of 1990, and oversight of he historic Fishery Conservation and Management Act of 1976. When he left the Congress in 1995, Rod Moore had left his mark on many bills passed by the House of Representatives and he was universally recognized for his encyclopedia knowledge of our nation's fishery laws.

Reflections of Rod Moore

I first met Don Young when I interviewed with him for a job in December 1976. I was a full time student at the University of Alaska Fairbanks and the day after the interview I had 4 final exams. The interview was in Anchorage so that morning I loaded up my textbooks and got on a plane to Anchorage, studying all the way. I met with Don and was impressed with him. He asked me honestly whether I could stand to be in DC for at least 2 years. I told him that I had come to Alaska from DC, where I was stationed in the Marine Corps, and 2 years was about the right amount of time. We must have hit it off because he not only hired me but the two years turned into nearly 18.

Later on, I learned that my competition for the job was somebody from Seattle who was being pushed by Jack Ferguson, Don's administrative assistant, and he was asking for a salary that was $500 per year more than I was (a reasonable amount of money at the time). I jokingly accused Don of hiring me because I would work cheaper. Don grinned but never denied it.

Over the years, I found Don to be a wonderful man to work for; he was as much of a friend as he was a boss. In spite of his gruff exterior, his tough talk, his deliberate country boy mannerisms (including his habit of cleaning his nails with a large Buck knife while sitting in committee), he could be tender and caring. I once watched him take on Newt Gingrich, the Minority Whip in the House, refusing to call for a series of protest roll call votes because Walter Jones Sr., the Chairman of the Merchant Marine and Fisheries Committee was ill and Don wanted to let him get off the floor of the House as quickly as possible. He became best friends with Rep. Gerry Studds (D-MA), a gay liberal Democrat. The two of them would go to

279

the floor and argue over hot button issues like gun control or abortion, then would return to Committee and vote in lock-step. During one of his final appearances on the floor of the House, Gerry jokingly offered an amendment to re-name the Magnuson-Stevens Fishery Conservation and Management Act as the "Young Studds Act" to commemorate the leaders in the house that originated the final bill.

Don is not an erudite man, often preferring to speak off the cuff rather than follow a written script. Over the years I learned to give him notes with just the essence of what he had to say; otherwise, in trying to read something he would get rushed and it wouldn't come out right. It was almost always better to brief him on the issue, maybe give him a couple of key phrases, then sit back and let him go. I can remember only two occasions when I had him read a speech I had written. I agonized over both of them for hours, getting the cadence just right, putting in commas where I wanted him to stop and take a breath, etc. I was surprised –and pleased – when he delivered them just as I wrote them, without hesitating, rushing through, or ad-libbing.

On the other hand, Don was famous for making retorts that delighted – and sometimes confused – his supporters. In a committee mark-up session on the Marine Mammal Protection Act, his response to a proposed amendment outlawing noise-making devices to scare porpoises away from tuna nets was, "a deaf dolphin is better than a dead dolphin." His classic response to an amendment restricting land use was, "You don't hunt rabbits on a pool table just because it's green," – a statement that makes sense when you think about it but one that befuddled supporters and opponents alike. At one point there was a collection of "Don Young-isms" floating around his office but it has disappeared over time.

Needless to say, Don doesn't like to take direction. During negotiations over a maritime bill, I got Don to agree to offer, then withdraw, an amendment. Come the day of subcommittee markup, I was sitting in the counsel's chair in front of the subcommittee. Don offered the amendment; the three Washington members of the subcommittee opposed it, and at that point Don was supposed to withdraw his amendment. But Don kept arguing in favor of it, causing angry glares to be directed at me by the Washington members and staff. I could do nothing, seated where I was. Finally, Don leaned over to Rep. John Breaux, the subcommittee chair, and said loud enough for me to hear: "Should I withdraw this?" Breaux responded: "Nah, I'll support you and I've got all the proxies." It passed and all I could do was shrug. Things were a bit tense for a while between my colleagues and me.

On another occasion, during a very tight campaign, we discovered that Mayor John Devens – Don's opponent who was gaining in the polls – had answered a questionnaire from the National Wildlife Federation in support of increasing regulations of wetlands in Alaska. This was a hot topic, with the majority of Alaskans avidly opposed to Devens' position. With a televised statewide debate coming up the next day, we scripted a series of questions for Don to ask Devens with the killer being "Why, then, did you support more wetlands regulation in response to a question from the National Wildlife Federation?" We knew that whatever response Devens gave he would look bad. Come the day of the debate, Don wandered into the campaign office telling everyone a joke he had just heard about a talking frog (which wasn't very funny). We got him back on track – or so we thought – and headed off to the debate. At the appropriate time, Don started off asking the questions that would have set up Devens for the kill, then suddenly grinned, and told the frog joke. Nobody understood what he was talking about, several people thought, it was not only not funny but also inappropriate, and we missed our chance at a runaway election victory (Don later won by a less than 1% margin). Don was appropriately - though not entirely - shamefaced.

The one person that Don would always listen to was Lu, his wife Lu had been his political partner, as well as his partner in life, since Don first ran for office as mayor of Fort Yukon. When I first met Lu in January 1977, we hit it off right away. She was a stay-at-home mom, looking after their two daughters. When she found out that I had lived in Fairbanks and spent my summers in a Native village, we discovered we had things to talk about. I adored Lu as much as I admired Don. There were those who claimed that Lu was too demanding, too autocratic, but that was a side of her that I never saw.

During his career, Don has been guided by his love for his family, his love for his state, and his principles. Looking back, I am proud and honored to have had the opportunity to work with him and – more important – to call him and his family my friends.

Upon becoming Chairman of the House Resources Committee on January 11, 1995, Don Young hired a number of talented men and women to assist in the operation of the Committee in the 104th Congress. One of those appointed was a young attorney who had lived in Anchorage and Fairbanks. He had also served for six years as a member of the Senior Staff for Alaska's Senator Ted Stevens.

283

Duane Gibson was highly recommended to the new Chairman of the Resources Committee. His legislative experience and knowledge of the State of Alaska and its key natural resources was invaluable. During the next six years, Duane played a key role in salvage timber sales, the Quincy Library Group Forest Recovery and Economic Stability Act, and the reform of the Wildlife and Sport Fish Restoration Programs. President William J. Clinton codified each of these major legislative efforts into federal law.

Duane was also the Staff Director of the Resource Committee's Oversight Office. In that capacity, he and his staff carefully investigated a number of questionable actions taken by agencies of the Clinton Administration.

After the highly successful six years as Chairman of the Resources Committee, Don Young was appointed Chairman of the House Transportation and Infrastructure Committee. Duane Gibson was hired as the Staff Director of the Subcommittee on Highways and Transit. His Subcommittee team was responsible for laying the groundwork that resulted in the historic passage of the Safe, Accountable, Flexible, Efficient Transportation Equity Act: A Legacy for Users.

Today, Duane is a successful consultant for The Livingston Group that is recognized as one of the most respected bipartisan government relations firms in the United States. As a lobbyist, he has helped to shepherd legislation dealing with the Energy Auto Loan Program, highway transportation programs for Native Americans, and liability caps on construction companies who responded to the 9/11 terrorist attacks. I will always remember Duane's important role in the Florida recount of the 2000 Presidential Election. From hanging chads, oversee the actions of the Clinton Administration, and helping to move legislation through the Congress for his clients, my friend Duane Gibson has always done a great job.

Reflections of Duane Gibson

Don Young is a rare type of Congressman. He is very real. He tells you what he thinks and does not shade what he says. He is a candid and frank person and in my opinion a rare and needed type of individual in politics and in the House of Representatives. Don was my Congressman before I worked for him. He is very reflective of most Alaskans.

My time with him was as his Counsel on the Committee on Resources. I remember how little power any Republican had while in the minority, but I also remember how that changed in January 1995 after the Republican sweep in November 1994. Don was finally in the majority, became the head

285

*of his Resources Committee and he
really stepped up to controlling and
directing the Committee. This is when
the Committee hired me. Don
reorganized the Committee and my role
was special projects and Alaska issues.*

*Our first project was the timber salvage
law. We held several hearings, a bunch
of meetings with different interests, and
wrote legislation to expedite the
harvesting of dead and dying timber.
Who could be against that idea? This
was not about cutting live trees. Don
had a Task Force with some of the new
Committee members from the west to
address that issue. Hearings were in
D.C. and also field hearings in the west.
Don led the effort and I remember the
members being hungry for action. They
wanted something positive to happen —
the forests to be cleared of dead trees
that would certainly burn and release
carbon and the lumber mills to get some
timber so people could work and the
industry might recover. The motivation
for the Task Force was to alleviate the
fears that had been caused by so many
forest fires. Yet, certain environmental
groups were "worried" to death about
global warming. As a result, they were
opposed to cutting and using dead and
dying trees, that ironically, if ignited
would release mega-tons of carbon.
Their intellectual dishonesty of these
groups was astonishing. They opposed
Don at all costs because they needed
something to oppose and they tried to*

demonize Don and his members in the process.

When we realized that the legislation, which truncated the timing of the environmental process and eliminated several levels of appeal of "salvage" timber sales to expedite those harvests would not easily get floor time due to the busy schedule, Don took our advice and we made move to attach the legislation to the Interior Appropriations bill. I will never forget going with Don into Chairman Bob Livingston's office to make the pitch to get this done. The notion suggested by Don Young that, "My members need action, accomplishments" carried the day with Bob. Bob said, "Well, if you have the votes to do it, then let's give it a try." We then began our campaign, organized the support, and got very favorable vote in the House of Representatives, making the legislation part of the Appropriations bill.

The language carried in the House and Senate Conference Committee and Don's members had their victory. Sadly, however, the Clinton Administration basically refused to use the new law. They slow rolled and dragged the process out while continuing to let the West burn. I cannot help to think that if the law had been properly followed and used over the ensuing years, the very devastating 2017 California wildfires would not have been so severe. Ironically, there were a bunch of groups in Southern California who funded the opposition groups who opposed us, lobbied against us, and demonized Don and his colleagues.

This is despite the fact that these fires were destroying their homes and business. Nevertheless, Don was very successful at getting that legislation passed and getting the job done for his members.

There are other timber issues that we worked over the years, like the Quincy Library Group timber bill--with the local environmentalists and the timber companies--only still to be opposed by the national environmental groups. It goes to demonstrate that the opposition industry is indeed an industry. Their cause was to be against Don Young and anything reasonable that Don sought, but we won the QLG bill too, with the help of Congressman Wally Herger and Senator Feinstein who at that time had enough of what the environmental community said.

My other role with Don was the Staff Director of the Oversight Office during the remaining 4 years on the Committee. In that role while Bill Clinton was still President, we investigated probably a dozen, maybe 20 actions taken by his Administration. Most were at the Interior Department. Don appointed Task Forces for some of

288

the issues: timber salvage, Grand Staircase Escalante Monument created under the Antiquities Act, several National Park Service issues, lots of stuff with the Council on Environmental Quality, the banking system as it was
used by the Clinton Administration to leverage private timberland preservation from a large timber company – Pacific Lumber owned by Charles Hurwitz. The report that I prepared on that issue was put in the Congressional Record at the end of Don's Chairmanship. I think we issued around 250 subpoenas. There were hearings, contempt procedures and anything we could do to slow down the often illegal and most questionable agenda-driven actions and decisions by the Clinton Administration zealots.

Don was also interested, as were his members, in the concept of devolution of power and land to the states. We made that point with a bill that I worked for him, to transition and transfer the entire Tongass National Forest to the State of Alaska. People loved it in Alaska and it reinforced what Don believed: that power closest to the people is best. It made the point that national decisions about local harvests of timber or use of fish or anything for that matter were rarely the best decisions and rarely grounded in true facts. Don was constantly fighting to help

289

people to understand that God-given resources are put there to manage and use, not rot and waste, and that federal policy ought to reflect the principle of the wise use of all natural resources.

I also served as the Staff Director of the Transportation and Infrastructure Subcommittee on Highways and Transit. It was my job to organize the Subcommittee for Chairman Don Young and to begin the reauthorization process for the next highway bill, which was enacted in 2005 as the SAFETEA-LU. I was at the Subcommittee for two years.

Over the eight years I worked for Don Young, I got to know him fairly well. While Don was sure a great personality, he is a very, very good person, too. He is honest and straightforward. You generally know what he is thinking because he does not shade telling you his thoughts. He cares passionately about Alaska and his constituents. He is very loyal. He keeps his word. He believes in God. These character traits and qualities served him very well when a flurry of investigations got near to him. There are takers in every institution, but Don Young is not and never will be one of those takers. He is a giver. He gives freely to Alaska and his constituents. He gives to his country and to the US House. The United States of America is a better place because Don Young has been the Congressman for All Alaska for over 45 years (23 terms). He is what is needed in Congress and I am extraordinarily proud that Don Young was my Congressman, my boss, my Chairman, and that he was and remains a friend.

If you visit a legislature in Austin, Juneau, Richmond, Sacramento or Washington, D.C., you will notice there are individuals promoting various legislative ideas. A significant number of those people are being paid for their services and have become known as lobbyists.

In our nation's capitol, many of these lobbyists are former Congressmen, former Senators, and former staff who work for the legislative branch of government. I had the pleasure of working with a handful of good folks who lacked this work experience but were superb representatives for their clients. One of those lobbyists was my friend Rick Marks who is a Principal at the Robertson, Monagle and Eastaugh (ROMEA) in Reston, Virginia. This firm has an extensive fisheries related client base.

Prior to joining the firm, Rick was a marine fish biologist for the State of North Carolina and a Fishery Reporting Specialist and Benthic Marine Field Technician for the National Oceanic and Atmospheric Administration. He holds a Master of Science Degree in Marine

Environmental Science and has written scientific peer-reviewed papers on marine finfish ecology and biology.

With a client list including the Alaska Groundfish Data Bank, California Wetfish Producers Association, Garden State Seafood Association, Organized Fishermen of Florida, Pacific States Marine Fisheries Commission, and the West Coast Seafood Processors Association, Rick was a frequent witness and visitor to our Subcommittee on Fisheries, Wildlife, Oceans and Insular Affairs. He was always welcomed and I am sure my colleagues Bonnie Bruce and Dave Whaley would agree that he was a first rate lobbyist for his clients. He also developed a personal relationship with the Congressman for All of Alaska.

Reflections of Rick Marks

As a natural resource lobbyist working for many years in Washington for the oldest firm from the State of Alaska I had the honor and privilege to work with and testify before Chairman Young on many occasions. My most memorable DY story comes not from the Halls of Congress but from the golf course – it encapsulates how he approached life, totally in the moment and utterly fearless. It was the late 90's, we were partners in a best ball tournament at the local course in Reston, Virginia. We were in a tight match and the Chairman was enjoying the challenge, chomping on a cigar, telling jokes, and swinging for the fences.

We were on the back nine in a close contest when we stopped the cart at our ball in the fairway for an approach shot to the green, the second on a Par 4. It was an unbelievably difficult shot, over sand with no green to work with and a downhill slope to the hole. There I am, standing over the ball with wedge in hand hopelessly trying to figure how to hit this shot and not embarrass myself in front of this larger-than-life Congressman when he looks at me wearing a Cheshire grin and quips, "Oh, just go ahead and hit it, God hates a coward!" Quintessential Don Young.

I made the shot and we sunk a very long twisting birdie putt to win the hole. He was absolutely jubilant! It was a really neat moment that reminds me of how this Congressional lion lived his life and served our Nation for so many years.

Don Young is now the longest serving Member of Congress from the State of Alaska. Along with former U.S. Senators Bob Bartlett, Ernest Gruening, and Ted Stevens, Don Young is one of the most important political leaders in the history of the 49th State. In fact, in a recent Anchorage Daily News article, his 2008 Democrat opponent, Anchorage Mayor

Ethan Berkowitz opined, "He's is the best politician that this state has ever produced."

During his illustrious career, Don Young has authored more public laws than any other Member in the modern era of the U.S. House of Representatives. This is the highest number by any Member in the history the U.S. House of Representatives and places him amongst other legislative giants like Henry Clay, John Dingell, Nicholas Longworth, and Sam Rayburn. Don Young has several times been named one of the most effective U.S. federal legislators. It is my hope that the Congress will recognize Don Young's huge impact on our nation's fisheries by renaming our premier federal law as the Magnuson-Stevens-Young Fishery Conservation and Management Act.

Don Young is a perfect representative of his state because his life experiences as a commercial fishermen, gold miner, logger, Native American teacher, trapper, tug and barge operator and river boat captain epitomizes the spirit of Alaska. As John Muir once wrote, "You should never go to Alaska as a young man because you'll never be satisfied with any other place as long as you live."

When I asked the Congressman for All of Alaska, why Alaska is such a special place, he said, "I have always felt like a school child that opened the largest box of candy and trying to decide what is the best piece. I have visited the entire state and Alaska is a place of breathtaking beauty, wonderful caring people, and it has been such a great honor to represent them in the United States Congress." The People of Alaska are blessed to have such a dedicated, hardworking, and successful public servant who works tirelessly every day to improve their lives.

It has been my great honor to work for and watch this legislative giant achieve results. In a day when bipartisanship is frequently disdained, Don Young is happy to work with any member of Congress regardless of their political affiliation or ideology. You can be sure that during those legislative negotiations, he will never forget that he is the Congressman for All of Alaska.

ACKNOWLEDGEMENTS

As I reflect upon the last year I have spent writing this book, it is clear that I would not have been as successful without the invaluable assistance of many people. I want them to know that I deeply appreciate their input, time, and encouragement.

I would first like to thank Brooke Daly who is a Legislative Reference Librarian at the State Capitol in Juneau, Alaska. Brooke was responsible for providing me with a print out of the bills sponsored and cosponsored by Don Young in the Alaska Legislature. I also want to thank Christina Bailey and Laura Hanson who are Senior Research Librarians at the Congressional Research Service; Rosemary Speranza who works at the University of Fairbanks Library; and Julie Stricker at the *Fairbanks Daily News Miner*.

Since a significant amount of Don Young's illustrious career occurred before the advent of the Internet, it would have been difficult, if not impossible, to read Congressional Records, Committee Reports, or Public Laws prior to 1995 without the assistance of the staff at the Library of Congress' Law Library and the William S. Hein Company. In particular, my thanks go to Sheila Jarrett who works for Hein and was extraordinarily kind to me. For anyone interested in doing research on the U.S. Congress or the U.S. federal government, Hein Online is an indispensable source.

I am also grateful for the invaluable insights of former Congressmen Jack Fields of Texas and Bill Brewster of Oklahoma, former Young staffers Duane Gibson, Jim Lexo and Rod Moore, and lobbyist Rick Marks. There is no question their reflections and stories made this a better book.

I would also like to thank members of my Marshall Writing Group. Twice a month, Rosemary Farquhar, Annette Lewis, Joy Schaya, Marie Simpson, and Elizabeth "Bess" Taylor carefully listen to my draft chapters and provide their suggested improvements in a kind manner. I am always pleased to obtain the valuable advice of these colleagues and friends. In particular, I want to add a special thank you to the leader of our group, Joy Schaya, who is not only an extremely talented writer but was willing to spend countless hours editing the final version of the book. This book is significantly better because of the time she was willing to dedicate. Joy your efforts were much appreciated.

No list of acknowledgements would be complete without a huge thank you to members of the Dean of the House of Representatives staff. In particular, this book would not have been written without the support of Chief of Staff Pam Day, former Communications Director Matt Shuckerow, and my friend Bruce Newman who never hesitated to provide me with exactly what I needed. If you enjoy the various pictures in this book, the person responsible for organizing them and getting them ready for publication was Bruce Newman. Thank you, Bruce. As I am sure Don Young would agree, very little gets done on Capitol Hill without the assistance of staff members. In the case of the Dean of the House, he is fortunate to have a superbly talented and outstanding staff in Washington D.C. and in his District Offices in Alaska. Many thanks for always taking my calls, responding to my emails, and assisting me in this project.

This book would also not have been written without the encouragement, love, and patience of my family. Gayle, Rick, Chris, Erin, Stacey, Mitchell, Elise, Kelly Dawn, and Christopher are what make life worth living for me. You are always in my heart.

Finally, it is no secret that I am computer challenged. This book simply wouldn't be published without the tremendous talents of my son Chris who was my designer, graphic artist, and marketing specialist who always took my calls even late at night with good humor and patience.

EXHIBITS

IMMEDIATE RELEASE   January 3, 1959

James C. Hagerty, Press Secretary to the President

- -

THE WHITE HOUSE

ADMISSION OF THE STATE OF ALASKA INTO THE UNION

- - - - - - - - - -

BY THE PRESIDENT OF THE UNITED STATES OF AMERICA

A PROCLAMATION

WHEREAS the Congress of the United States by the act approved on
July 7, 1958 (72 Stat. 339), accepted, ratified, and confirmed the
constitution adopted by a vote of the people of Alaska in an election held
on April 24, 1956, and provided for the admission of the State of Alaska
into the Union on an equal footing with the other States of the Union upon
compliance with certain procedural requirements specified in that act; and

WHEREAS it appears from information before me that a majority
of the legal votes cast at an election held on August 26, 1958, were in
favor of each of the propositions required to be submitted to the people of
Alaska by section 8 (b) of the act of July 7, 1958; and

WHEREAS it further appears from information before me that a
general election was held on November 25, 1958, and that the returns of
the general election were made and certified as provided in the act of
July 7, 1958; and

WHEREAS the Acting Governor of Alaska has certified to me the
results of the submission to the people of Alaska of the three propositions
set forth in section 8 (b) of the act of July 7, 1958, and the results of the
general election; and

WHEREAS I find and announce that the people of Alaska have duly
adopted the propositions required to be submitted to them by the act of
July 7, 1958, and have duly elected the officers required to be elected by
that act:

NOW, THEREFORE, I, DWIGHT D. EISENHOWER, President of
the United States of America, do hereby declare and proclaim that the
procedural requirements imposed by the Congress on the State of Alaska
to entitle that State to admission into the Union have been complied with
in all respects and that admission of the State of Alaska into the Union on
an equal footing with the other States of the Union is now accomplished.

IN WITNESS WHEREOF, I have hereunto set my hand and caused
the Seal of the United States of America to be affixed.

301

Rep. Don Young's Laws Enacted
Alaska State Legislature
1967-1973

House Bills: Sponsor

- HB 428
  - Small Grain Incentive Program
    Ch. 55 SLA 1970

- HB 601
  - Construction and Equipping Libraries in Rural Communities
    Ch. 42 SLA 1970

- HB 602
  - Appropriation to State Libraries
    Ch. 94 SLA 1970

- HB 689
  - Regulations and Certification of Air Carriers
    Ch. 203 SLA 1968

Senate Bills: Sponsor

- SB 70
  - Dental Insurance Coverage Under State's Group Insurance Plan
    Ch. 46 SLA 1973

- SB   123
  - Detention of Suspected Shoplifters
    Ch. 111 SLA 1971

- SB   169
  - Teacher's Retirement Survivor's Allowance
    Ch.52 SLA 1972

- SB   325
  - Benefits Under Teacher's Retirement Services
    Ch. 184 SLA 1972

- SB   346
  - Notary Public Seals
    Ch. 17 SLA 1972

House Bills: Co-Sponsor

- HB   2
  - Governance of the Department of Education
    Ch. 96 SLA 1967

- HB   13
  - State Aid for Agricultural Fairs
    Ch. 97 SLA 1967

- HB   37
  - Bonus for Discovery and Production of Certain Mineral Ores
    Ch. 98 SLA 1967

- HB 127
  - Public Defender Agency
    Ch. 109 SLA 1969

- HB 346
  - Voter Qualifications
    Ch. 15 SLA 1970

- HB 412
  - Raising the Agricultural
    Revolving Loan Fund
    Authorization
    Ch. 81 SLA 1970

- HB 413
  - Appropriation to
    Department of Natural
    Resources
    Ch. 149 SLA 1970

Senate Bills: Co-Sponsor

- SB 41
  - Counsel and Advice to
    Persons in Emotional Crisis
    Ch. 119 SLA 1971

- SB 144
  - Endangered Species of Fish
    and Wildlife
    Ch. 115 SLA 1971

- SB 153
  - Rules of Criminal Procedures
    Ch. 126 SLA 197

- SB 195
  - Tax on Watercraft Fuel
    Ch. 124 SLA 1971

- SB 290
  - Teachers Retirement Salaries
    Ch. 44 SLA 1972

- SB 298
  - State Matching Funds for
    Construction of Sports
    Facilities
    Ch. 155 SLA 1972

- SB 308
  - Assignment of Teachers
    Ch. 53 SLA 1972

- SB 318
  - Adopt Uniform Alcoholism
    and Intoxication Treatment
    Act
    Ch. 207 SLA 1972

- SB 337
  - Agricultural and Industrial
    Fairs
    Ch. 154 SLA 1972

CONGRESSMAN DON YOUNG
INTRODUCED BILLS
PUBLIC LAWS: 1973-2018

(1). Document *Miss Keku* as Vessel of the United States to Engage in Fisheries.
04/17/73, Public Law 93-66.

(2). Relief of Michael A. Korhonen
07/12/74, Public Law 93-83.

(3). Amend Alaska Native Claims Settlement Act to allow Cook Inlet Land Exchange
11/15/77, Public Law 95-178.

(4). Relief of the City of Nenana, Alaska
08/14/79, Public Law 96-55.

(5). Cook Inlet Land Exchange
07/17/80, Public Law 96-311.

(6). Allow Enrollment of Metlakatia Indian Community
12/05/80, Public Law 96-505.

(7). Convey certain lands in Alaska comprising manufacturing site A056802
10/15/82, Public Law 97-340.

(8). Relief of Stephen C. Ruks
11/02/83, Public Law 98-4.

(9). Fur Seal Act Amendments of 1983
10/14/83, Public Law 98-129.

(10). Barrow Gas Field Transfer Act of 1984
07/17/84, Public Law 98-366.

(11). Amend Section 504 of Alaska
National Interest Lands Conservation Act
01/09/86, Public Law 99-235.

(12). Amend Section 901 of Alaska
National Interest Lands Conservation Act
03/19/86, Public Law 99-258.

(13). Haida Land Exchange Act of 1986
11/17/86, Public Law 99-664.

(14). Alaska Native Claims Settlement Act
02/03/88, Public Law 100-241.

(15). Amend Alaska National Interests
Lands Conservation Act – Submerged
Lands
08/16/88, Public Law 100-395.

(16). Modification of Boundaries of Alaska
Maritime National Wildlife Refuge
11/21/90, Public Law 101-622.

(17). Alaska Land Status Technical
Correction Act
10/14/92, Public Law 102-415.

(18). Kenai Natives Equity Act
10/23/92, Public Law 102-458.

(19). Koniag Lands Conveyance
Amendments of 1991
10/24/92, Public Law 102-489.

(20). Temporarily Extend Provisions of
Marine Mammal Protection Act
03/31/94, Public Law 103-228.

(21). Alaska Native Claims Settlement Act
– Cook Inlet Region Common Stock
05/18/95, Public Law 104-10.

(22). Hawaiian Home Lands Recovery Act
11/02/95, Public Law 104-42.

(23). Fisheries Act of 1995
11/03/95, Public Law 104-43.

(24). Greens Creek Land Exchange Act
04/01/96, Public Law 104-123

(25). Technical Corrections to Federal Oil
and Gas Royalty Management Act
09/22/96, Public Law 104-200.

(26). Study of Joint Federal-State
Commission on Alaska Natives
10/09/96, Public Law 104-270.

(27). Indian Health Care Improvement Act
10/19/96, Public Law 104-313.

(28). Omnibus Parks and Public Lands
Management Act
11/12/96, Public Law 104-333.

(29). National Wildlife Refuge System
Improvement Act of 1997
10/09/97, Public Law 105-57.

(30). Hood Bay Land Exchange Act
10/10/97, Public Law 105-60.

(31). African Elephant Conservation
Reauthorization Act of 1988
    08/05/98, Public Law 105-217.

(32). Native Americans Technical
Corrections Act
    10/14/98, Public Law 105-256.

 (33). Glacier Bay National Park Boundary
Adjustment Act
    10/30/98, Public Law 105-317.

(34). ANCSA Land Bank Protection Act
    10/31/98, Public Law 105-333.

(35). Coastwise Privileges for *M/V Mist
Cove*
    07/06/00, Public Law 106-5.

(36). Bikini Resettlement and Relocation
Act of 2000
    04/28/00, Public Law 106-188.

(37). Amend Alaska Natives Claims
Settlement Act – Elim Native Corporation
    05/02/00, Public Law 106-194.

(38). Fish and Wildlife Programs
Improvement and National Wildlife
Refuge
    System Centennial Act
    11/01/00, Public Law 106-408.

(39). Fishermen's Protective Act
Amendments
    11/07/00, Public Law 106-450.

(40). Herbert H. Bateman Educational and Administrative Center
    11/09/00, Public Law 106-400

(41). Governing International Fishing Agreement
    12/23/00, Public Law 106-562.

(42). Air Transportation Safety and System Stabilization Act
    09/22/01, Public Law 107-42.

(43). John F. Kennedy Center Plaza Authorization Act
    09/18/02, Public Law 107-224.

(44). Amend Section 5307 of Title 49 – Transit Systems
    10/01/02, Public Law 107-232.

(45). Pipeline Safety Improvement Act
    12/17/02, Public Law 107-355.

(46). Russian River Land Act
    12/19/02, Public Law 107-362.

(47). Hydrographic Services Improvement Act Amendments
    12/19/02, Public Law 107-372.

(48). Surface Transportation Extension Act
    09/30/03, Public Law 108-88.

(49). Vision 100 – Century of Aviation Reauthorization Act
    12/12/03, Public Law 108-176.

(50). Surface Transportation Extension Act, Part II
    02/29/04, Public Law 108-202.

(51). Surface Transportation Extension Act, Part III
    06/30/04, Public Law 108-263.

(52). Surface Transportation Extension Act, Part IV
    07/30/04, Public Law 108-280.

(53). Coast Guard and Maritime Transportation Act
    08/09/04, Public Law 108-293.

(54). Capetown Treaty Implementation Act
    08/09/04, Public Law 108-297.

(55). Surface Transportation Extension Act, Part V
    09/30/04, Public Law 108-310

(56). John F. Kennedy Center Reauthorization Act
    10/30/04, Public Law 108-410.

(57). Norman Y. Mineta Research and Special Programs Reauthorization Act
    11/30/04, Public Law 108-426.

(58). Surface Transportation Extension Act
    05/31/05, Public Law 109-14.

(59). Surface Transportation Extension Act, Part II
    07/01/05, Public Law 109-20.

(60). Surface Transportation Extension Act, Part III
07/20/05, Public Law 109-35.

(61). Surface Transportation Extension Act, Part IV
07/22/05, Public Law 109-37.

(62). Surface Transportation Extension Act, Part V
07/28/05, Public Law 109-40.

(63). Surface Transportation Extension Act, Part VI
07/30/05, Public Law 109-42.

(64). SAFETEA-LU
08/10/05, Public Law 109-59.

(65). Sportfishing and Recreational Boating Safety Amendments Act
09/29/05, Public Law 109-74.

(66). Coast Guard Hurricane Relief Act
12/22/05, Public Law 109-141.

(67). Coast Guard and Maritime Transportation Act
07/12/06, Public Law 109-241.

(68). Railroad Retirement Technical Improvement Act
10/06/06, Public Law 109-305.

(69). National Transportation Safety Board Reauthorization Act
12/21/06, Public Law 109-443.

(70). Pipeline Inspection, Protection, Enforcement, and Safety Act
        12/29/06, Public Law 109-468.

(71). Railroad Retirement Disability Earnings Act
        01/12/07, Public Law 109-478.

(72). Multinational Species Conservation Funds Reauthorization Act
        12/06/07, Public Law 110-132.

(73) Designate Robert Boochever United States Courthouse in Juneau
        10/05/12, Public Law 112-187.

(74). Conveyance of Property to Maniilaq Association in Kotzebue, Alaska
        01/14/13, Public Law 112-263.

(75). Vietnam Veterans Donor Acknowledge Act
        07/18/13, Public Law 113-21.

(76). Alaska Native Tribal Health Consortium Land Transfer Act
        12/26/13, Public Law 113-68.

(77). Huna Tlingit Traditional Gull Egg Use Act
        07/25/14, Public Law 113-142.

(78). Disapproval of Department of Interior Rule Affecting National Wildlife Refuges in Alaska
        04/03/17, Public Law 115-20.

(79). Indian Employment, Training and
Related Services Consolidation Act
     12/18/17, Public Law 115-93.

(80). Swan Lake Hydroelectric Project
Boundary Correction Act
     07/20/18, Public Law 115-200.

(81). Terror Lake Hydroelectric Project
Authorization Act
     07/20/18, Public Law 115-201.

.

.

CONGRESSMAN DON YOUNG SPONSORED BILLS INCLUDED IN HOUSE OR SENATE MEASURES PUBLIC LAWS: 1973-2018

(1). Direct Secretary of the Interior to sell certain lands to Gospel Missionary Union
12/31/74, Public Law 93-103. (S. 184)

(2). Amend Section 607 (K) 8 of Merchant Marine Act of 1936.
10/01/73, Public Law 93-116. (S. 902)

(3). Alaska Native Claims Settlement Act Amendments
01/02/76, Public Law 94-204. (S. 1469)

(4). Established Klondike Gold Rush National Historic Park in Alaska and Washington
06/30/76, Public Law 94-223. (S. 98)

(5). Relief of Jerry L. Crow
01/03/83, Public Law 97-49. (S. 835)

(6). Designating January 3, 1984 as Alaska Statehood Day
06/22/83, Public Law 98-42. (S.J.Res. 42)

(7). Arctic Research and Policy Act
07/31/84, Public Law 98-373. (S. 373)

(8). October 1985 as National Community College Month
10/22/85, Public Law 99-128. (S.J.Res. 158)

315

(9). Allow Alaskan Natives to Qualify for Wastewater Treatment Assistance
11/01/88, Public Law 100-581. (H.R. 2677)

(10). Coast Guard Compliance Act
12/12/89, Public Act 101-225 (H.R. 2459)

(11). Prince William Sound Oil Spill Response Act of 1989
08/18/90, Public Law 101-380. (H.R. 1465)

(12). Aleutian Trade Act
11/16/90, Public Law 101-440. (H.R. 4009)

(13). Clear Impediments for Licensing of *M/V Pumpkin* for Coastwise Trade
11/16/90, Public Law 101-595. (H.R. 4009)

(14). Greens Creek Exchange Act
11/28/90, Public Law 101-626. (H.R. 987)

(15). Marine Resources Support Act
11/28/90, Public Law 101-627. (H.R. 2061)

(16). Clear Licensing Impediments for vessel *Cutty Sark*
08/17/91, Public Law 102-100. (H.R. 1006)

(17). Clear Licensing Impediments for vessel *M/V Nushagak*
08/17/91, Public Law 102-100. (H.R. 1006)

(18). International Fish and Wildlife Protection Act
11/02/92, Public Law 102-582. (H.R. 2152)

(19). North Pacific Anadromous Stocks Act of 1992
11/02/92, Public Law 102-587. (H.R. 5617)

(20). Provide Documentation to vessel
Yupik Star
11/04/92, Public Law 102-587. (H.R. 5617)

(21). Authorize Certification of Documentation for vessel *Grizzly Processor*
12/20/93, Public Law 103-206. (H.R. 2150)

(22). High Seas Fishing Compliance Act
11/03/95, Public Law 104-43. (H.R. 716)

(23). Sea of Okhotsk Fisheries Enforcement Act
11/03/95, Public Law 104-43. (H.R. 716)

(24). Alaska Power Administration Sale Act
11/28/95, Public Law 104-58. (S. 395)

(25). Mollie Beattie Alaska Wilderness Area Act
07/29/96, Public Law 104-167. (S. 1899)

(26). Fishery Conservation and Management Amendments of 1995
11/12/96, Public Law 104-297. (S. 39)

(27). Sikes Act Improvement Amendments
11/18/97, Public Law 105-85. (H.R. 1119)

(28). Migratory Bird Treaty Reform Act
10/30/98, Public Law 105-312. (H.R. 2807)

(29). Rhinoceros and Tiger Conservation Reauthorization Act
10/30/98, Public Law 105-312. (H.R. 2807)

(30). Coastwise Endorsement for vessel *FJORDING*
11/13/98, Public Law 105-383. (H.R. 2204)

(31). Coastwise Endorsement for vessel *Pacific Monarch*
11/13/98, Public Law 105-383. (H.R. 2204)

(32). Fisheries Survey Vessel Authorization Act
11/07/00, Public Law 106-450. (H.R. 1651)

(33). Yukon River Salmon Act
11/07/00, Public Law 106-450. (H.R. 1651)

(34). Neotropical Migratory Bird Conservation Act
07/20/00, Public Law 106-247. (S. 148)

(35). Airport Security Federalization Act
11/19/01, Public Law 107-71. (S. 1447)

(36). Railroad Retirement and Survivors' Improvement Act
12/21/01, Public Law 107-90. (H.R. 10)

(37). Appalachian Regional Development Reauthorization Act
03/12/02, Public Law 107-149. (S. 1206)

(38). Ratify Agreement between the Aleut Corporation and U.S. on Adak Island
10/11/02, Public Law 107-239. (S. 1325)

(39). Omnibus Maritime Improvements Act
11/25/02, Public Law 107-295. (S. 1214)

(40). Maritime Transportation and Anti-Terrorism Act
11/25/02, Public Law 107-295. (S. 1214)

(41). Coast Guard Personnel and Maritime Safety Act
11/25/02, Public Law 107-295. (S. 1214)

(42). Coast Guard Authorization Act for Fiscal Year 2002
11/25/02, Public Law 107-295. (S. 1214)

(43). Maritime Policy Improvement Act
11/25/02, Public Law 107-295. (S. 1214)

(44). Arming Pilots against Terrorism Act
11/25/02, Public Law 107-296. (H.R. 5005)

(45). National Oceanic and Atmospheric Administration Commissioned Officer Corps Act
12/19/02, Public Law 107-372. (H.R. 4883)

(46). National Transportation Safety Board Reauthorization Act
12/06/03, Public Law 108-168. (S. 579)

(47). Emergency Directed Rail Service Act
01/23/04, Public Law 108-199. (H.R. 2673)

(48). Craig Recreation Land Purchase Act
10/13/04, Public Law 108-325. (S. 1778)

(49). Alaska Native Allotment Subdivision Act
10/18/04, Public Law 108-337. (S. 1421)

(50). Alaska Native Claims Settlement Act – Common Stock
03/13/06, Public Law 109-179. (S. 449)

(51). Wright Amendment Reform Act
10/13/06, Public Law 109-352. (S. 3661)

(52). Alaska Water Resources Act of 2007
05/08/08, Public Law 110-229. (S. 2739)

(53). Denali National Park and Alaska Railroad Exchange Act
05/08/08, Public Law 110-229. (S. 2739)

(54). Convey Parcel of Real Property to Alaskan Railroad Corporation
06/06/08, Public Law 110—244. (H.R. 1195)

(55). Hydrographic Services Improvement Act Amendments
10/10/08, Public Law 110-386. (S. 1582)

(56). Mount Stevens and Ted Stevens Icefield Act
10/18/10, Public Law 111-284. (S. 3802)

(57). Designate James M. Fitzgerald United States Courthouse in Anchorage
03/14/12, Public Law 112-101 (S. 1710)

(58). Salmon Lake Land Selection
Resolution Act
 06/15/12, Public Law 112-133. (S. 292)

(59). Maritime Lien Reform Act
 12/20/12, Public Law 112-213. (H.R. 2838)

(60). Denai National Park Improvement
Act
 09/18/13, Public Law 113-33. (S. 157)

(61). Anchorage Land Conveyance Act
 12/19/14, Public Law 113-291. (H.R. 3979)

(62). American Energy Independence and
Job Creation Act
 12/22/17, Public Law 115-97. (H.R. 1)

STAFF OF THE CONGESSMAN FOR ALL OF ALASKA

Personal Office Staff: 1973-2018

Jimmy Adams
Lynn Ager
Richard Agnew
Cynthia A. Ahwinona
Marilyn Alexander
Betty Almquist
*Michael Anderson
Coreen Armstrong
Peggy Arness
Christian Banner
Teresa Bell
Caroline Bickel
Michelle Blackwell
Steve Bolerjack
Rhonda Boyles
Levon Boyagian
Stuart Boyton
Cleatus Brislin
Terrance Brown
Bonnie B. Bruce
Pamela Buckley
Larry Burton
*Colin Chapman
Royce Chapman
Freddie Cipra
Sally Christian
Diane Church
Paula Conru
Dennis Cowels
Holly Croft

Jean Davin
Chuck Davis
*Pamela Day
Walter Deane
Michael V. DeFilippis
Ross Dietrich
Roslyn Eaton
Sandy Edwards
Erik Elam
Lorraine Elde
Lorraine Erickson
*Jack Ferguson
Christopher Fluhr
Lee Forsgren
Kim Fouch
Adrienne Franco
Kristine Frenge
Charlotte Garver
Ann Gibson
Bonnie Golden
Wesley Gregg
Carol Gustafson
Diane Hall
Steve Hansen
Alan Hartig
Frank Hausman
Michael Henry
Laurie Herman
Virginia A. Heyerdahl
Matthew Hite
Mary Hiratsuka
Jerry Hood
Mary Jo Hobbs
William P. Horn
Lucy Hudson
Rebecca Hultberg
Amy Inaba
Torry Irving

Jakob Johnsen
Mark Johnson
*Lloyd Jones
Greg Kaplan
William Kelder
*Art Kennedy
Kevin Kennedy
Meredith Kenny
Daniel Kish
Pamela Kish
Allison Klukas
Lillian Lahmeyer
Nicole LaPorte
Scott Leathard
*James W. Lexo, Jr.
Lanien Livingston
Daniel Logan
Terri London
Murphy McCollough
Connie McKenzie
Kelly Merrick
Luke Miller
Paul Milotte
Denise Mitstifer
Rod Moore
Eleanor Gray Mullen
Anne Mullins
Taylor Nelson
Martha Newell
Bruce Newman
Grace Nichols
Roberta Norman
Patricia O'Keefe
William T. O'Malley
Eleanor-Gray Mullen
Azabel Ordaz
Alexander Ortiz
Chad Padgett

Sarah Parsons
Byron Patterson
Laura Payne
Catherine Petty
Jeffrey Powers
Jeremy Price
Lisa Purrington
Aprille C. Raabe
John H. Ralston
Truman Reed
Stephen Renna
Josh Revak
Ellen Ring
Coreen Ritchie
Tara Risinger
*G. Maxwell Rohm
Robert Robenalt
Helen Ryan
Thomas Ryan
Douglas Salik
Matt Shuckerow
Jessica Scallon
Jackie Schaffer
Grant Schultz
William Sharrow
Richard Shephard
Jessica Siciliano
Linda Simpson
John Sloat
Sherrie Slick
Jeff Small
Jeff Smith
Michael Songer
Justin Sprinzen
Maxine Stanley
Nikki Steube
Kimberly Stickler
Gerri Sumpter

Jason Suslavich
Jessica Sweeney
Taniko Taylor
Greg Thom
Grant Thompson
Maude Tierney
Ann Vayda
Edith Vivian
Jesse von Stein
Mary Ann Wessels
Alana Wilson
Kelli Winebarger
Jennifer Wise
Nick Worthington
*Curtis (CJ) Zane

Committee on Resources: 1995-2000

Cynthia A. Ahwinona
Kathy Benedetto
Sharla F. Bickley
Bonnie B. Bruce
Chris Burroughs
Harry F. Burroughs
Debroah A. Callis
Thomas D. Casey
Laura Chamberlain
Kurt Christensen
William Condit
Kathy Cook
Michael Correia
Douglas Crandall
Dawn M. Criste
James Davin
Christina Delmont
David G. Dye
Robert C. Faber
Zachary Falcon

Theresa Fierro
Christopher Fluhr
Allen D. Freemeyer
Douglas Fuller
Duane R. Gibson
Nadina Gideon
Timothy W. Glidden
Gary Griffith
Jose M. Guillen
Steven M. Hansen
Mary Anne Harper
Anne E. Heissenbuttel
Michael K. Henry
Stephen Hodapp
Aloysius Hogan
Robert Howarth
Todd Hull
Kathy Crook Jarmiolowski
*Lloyd A. Jones
Christopher B. Kearney
Christine A. Kennedy
*Daniel V. Kish
Jason Knox
Nancy Laheeb
Linda Livingston
Katherine Lowry
Joshua Johnson
Joseph Love
Sharon McKenna
T.E. Manase Mansur
Brooke Mason
Elizabeth R. Megginson
Christina Meyer
*Brian Miller
Kathleen A. Miller
Andrea Nagy
Karen Needy
Natalie Nelson

Lisa Pittman
John Ramage
John Clark Rayfield
Pauline Reeping
Jeffrey Ripp
John C. Rishel
Veronica Rolocut
Lisa Diane Rulli
Sharon Cherie Sexton
Arturo Silva
William M. Simmons
Dan Smith
Michelle Sparck
Marcia M. Stewart
Jim Streeter
Curtis W. Thayer
Marion Tucker
Michael Twinchek
Sophia Varnasidis
Valerie S. West
David S. Whaley
Kyle Weaver
Jay Wiley
Shane Winfrey
Margherita T. Woods
Ann C. Yogt

Committee on Transportation and Infrastructure – 2001-2006

John Anderson
Sharon Barkeloo
William Barnes
Alexis Barrios
Geoff Bauman
Stephen Beaulieu
Jim Berard
William Bland

Susan Bodine
Winn Bott
Levon Boyagian
John Brennan
John Bressler
Chris C. Brown
Chris A. Burroughs
Debbie Callis
Donna Campbell
Marsha Canter
Huge Carroll
Fess Cassels
Bill Cody
James Coon
Tom Corcoran
Kris Demirjian
Rebecca Dye
Bailey Edwards
Blake Edwards
Raga Elim
Robert Faber
William Fox
Gilda Fuentez
Duane Gibson
Joseph Graziano
Jennifer Hall
Steven M. Hansen
Justin Harclerode
Christopher Hewitt
Reagan Highfill
Graham Hill
*Lloyd A. Jones
Travis Johnson
Christine Kennedy
Michael Kirlin
Russ Kline
Edward Lee
Holly E. Woodruff Lyons

Cheryl McCullough
Dan Matthews
Phillip Maxwell
Elizabeth Megginson
Derek Miller
Jimmy Miller
Ray Morales
Tracy G. Mosebey
Eric Nagel
Susan Newhouse
Amanda Newman
Jonathan Pawlow
John Clark Rayfleld
Jason Rosa
Joyce Rose
Solia Salinas
Kimberlee Saranko
Kevin Sard
Glenn Scammel
David Schaffer
John Scheib
Dan Schulman
Gilda Shirley
Justin Sprinzen
Richard Stanton
Adam Tsao
Melissa Theriault
Sonia Tutiven
James Tymon
Matt Wallen
Amy Warder
Fraser Verrusio
Charles Yessaian
Mark Zachares
Charles Ziegler
* Chief of Staffs

July 31, 2012

The HONORABLE Don Young
Congressman for All Alaska
Washington, DC

Dear Chairman Young:

Politicians often have a host of people thanking them for one thing or another. There is no shortage of people who have thanked you over the many years you have served Alaskans, because you have helped so many.

But I want to say thank you for something unrelated for what you have done as a Congressman. I want to say, "Thank you for being Don Young!"

I once gave a toast to you in California. I said that when someone became an elected official, he got to use the title "Honorable," in front of his name. But in your case, my toast went, the title "Honorable" is most apt and fitting for you, not because you were elected as Congressman for All Alaska, but rather, because of *who you are as a person* and how you conduct yourself with your family, your friends, your staff and your constituents. Don Young is an honorable man because of his core values and how he conducts himself, I said as we raised a glass to you.

You are Honorable because you pull your values from what God teaches and from common sense. You are true and honest. You do not lie to people and you treat people how you want to be treated. You are loyal, probably one of the most loyal people I know. This was so evident in your relationship with Lu. You treated her so well no matter what as you practiced what God said: "Husbands, love your wives..." You loved her with grace and sincerity. Everyone saw that. It showed what kind of person you are. Your loyalty was also evident in how you treated your staff and your friends and it is appreciated by all of us. You are absolutely genuine and straightforward. Your agenda is what you say it is and you say what it is in very plain language. Some might call that being direct. Some might call that being candid. I call that refreshing, particularly for an elected official. You want people to understand and you do not try to conceal—again because you are true and honest. These are the things I am thankful for about your character. These are things I have seen throughout the past 25 years as your constituent, your staff, your campaigner, and a friend. These are things that we need more of in our society.

So on this occasion that causes us to look back and reflect, **I thank you for being Don Young!** You taught me much, not only by what you said, but more importantly by what you did and how you conducted yourself. Your solid, core values and honest ways have served you well in good and times and times that were not so good. If only more politicians were like you, the Congress and our nation would be a better place.

All my best,

Duane R. Gibson

SOURCES

Foreword: The Last Frontier

Alaska.gov/visitors. Home

Borneman, Walter R., Alaska: Saga of a Bold Land, *Harper Collins*, 2003.

Clinton, Susan, The Story of Seward's Folly, *Regensteiner Publishing Enterprises, Inc.*, 1987.

Ragan, John David, The Explorers of Alaska, *Chelsea House Publications*, 1992.

Michener, James A., *Alaska, Random House*, 1988.

Newton, Jim, Eisenhower: The White House Years, *Doubleday*, 2011.

Oachs, Emily Rose, Exploring the States: Alaska: The Last Frontier, *Bellwether Media, Inc.*, 2014. *E*

Cooper, Bryan, Alaska: The Last Frontier, *William Morrow and Company, Inc.*, 1973.

The Alaska Almanac: Facts about Alaska, *Alaska Northwest Books*, 2006.

Seder, Isaac, Alaska: The Last Frontier, World Almanac Library, 2003.

Vincent, Carol Hardy, Federal Land Stewardship Overview and Data, CRS, December 29, 2014.

Chapter 1: Fort Yukon's Favorite Son

Jacobs, Deborah, The Caribous and Alaskan Oil, *PERC Reports*, Vol. 19, Number 2, June 2001.

Environmental Effects of the Alaska Pipeline, University of Michigan, 2013.

U.S. Court blocks permits to build Alaskan pipeline, *Reuters*, February 10, 1973.

Remarks of Congressman Gerald R. Ford on the Floor of the House of Representatives regarding the Alaskan Pipeline, August 2, 1973.

Porcupine Caribou Herd Shows Growth, Alaska Department of Fish and Game, March 2, 2011.

Clifton, L. J., and Gallaway, B. J., History of Trans Alaskan Pipeline System.

Aircraft Crash Database, National Aviation Administration, www.ntsb.gov.

Pipeline Facts, www.alyeska.pipe.com.

State of Alaska Official Returns, General Election, November 8, 1966, Secretary of State, Juneau, Alaska.

State of Alaska Official Returns, General Election, November 15, 1968, Secretary of State, Juneau, Alaska.

State of Alaska Official Returns, General Election, November 3, 1970, Secretary of State, Juneau, Alaska.

State of Alaska Official Returns, General Election, November 7, 1972, Secretary of State, Juneau, Alaska.

Don Young Bill Sponsorship Examples, Alaska State Legislature, 1967-1973, State Library, Alaska State Legislature, Juneau, Alaska.

Background on the Arctic Winter Games, *http://arctic.wintergames.org*.

Statement by Congressman Don Young on the floor of the House of Representatives Concerning H.R. 6540, Arctic Winter Games , *Congressional Record*, April 9, 1973, Page H11432.

Statement by Congressman Bill Young on the floor of the House of Representatives Concerning H.R. 6540, Arctic Winter Games, *Congressional Record*, March 14, 1973, Page H7678.

Chapter 2: Endangered Species Act

Carson, Rachel, *Silent Spring*, Houghton Mifflin, 1962.

www.who.int/mediacenters.

www.cdc.gov, DDT: Government Fact
Sheet, National Pesticide Information
Center.

Bohler, J. L. King, FW, the Audubon
Society Field Guide to North American
Reptiles and Amphibians, 1979.

Statement by Secretary of the Interior
Bruce Babbitt at Senate Environment and
Public Works Committee, April 22, 1999.

Statement by U.S. Fish and Wildlife
Service Director Jaime Clarke at Senate
Environment and Public Works
Committee, May 1999.

Smith, A. Robert, Our Don is 6th Young,
Anchorage Daily News, March 14, 1973.

Statement by Congressman Don Young on
the floor of the House of Representatives
Concerning H.R. 1467, Authorizing
Appropriations for the Endangered
Species Act of 1973, *Congressional Record,*
December 17, 1987, Page 36091.

Statement by Congressman Don Young on
the floor of the House of Representatives
Concerning Conference Report to H.R.
1467, *Congressional Record,* September 26,
1988, Page 25480.

Endangered Species Act of 1973:
Appropriations Authorizations for Fiscal
Years 1988-1992, P. L. 100-478, October 7,
1988.

Statement by Congressman Wayne Gilchrest on the floor of the House of Representatives Concerning H.R. 1588, National Defense Authorization Act, *Congressional Record,* May 22, 2003, Page H4410.

Oversight Hearing on Nonindigenous Species, Subcommittee on Fisheries, Wildlife, and Oceans, July 8, 1996.

Digest of Federal Resource Laws of Interest to the U.S. Fish and Wildlife Service.

A History of the Endangered Species Act of 1973, U.S. Fish and Wildlife Service, www.fws.gov.

ECOS Environmental Conservation Online System, U.S. Fish and Wildlife Service, Delisted Species, May 2, 2017.

History of the Endangered Species Act, www.ti.org.

Endangered and Threatened Species Conservation Act of 1973, Committee on Merchant Marine and Fisheries, July 27, 1973, Report No. 93-412.

A bill to strengthen the Endangered Species Act, *Congressional Record,* January 11, 1973, Page 72.

First Species Listed as Endangered, www.fws.gov.

Statement by Congressman Doc Hastings on the floor of the House of Representatives Concerning H.R. 4315, 21st Century Endangered Species Transparency Act, *Congressional Record,* July 29, 2014, Page H7007.

Chapter 3: America's Fish

Kurlansky, Mark, The Last Fish Tale, *Ballantine Books*, 2008.

Dolin, Eric Jay, Leviathan: The History of Whaling in America, W. W. Norton and Company, 2007.

Cooper, Michael L, Jamestown 1607. *Holiday House*, 2007.

Edwards, Judith, Jamestown, John Smith and Pocahontas, *Enslow Publishers, Inc.,* 2002.

Evans, Michael, Fishing, *Earth Times,* June 3, 2011, www.earthtimes.org.

Thompson, Kalee, Unacceptable Risk: Why Commercial Fishing is the Deadliest Job in America, *Popular Mechanics,* October 7, 2010.

Fisheries Economies of the United States 2015, U.S. Department of Commerce, May 2017.

Pedrosa, Carmen N., How the 200 Nautical Miles Limit Evolved, *The Philippines Star*, February 3, 2013.

Murawski, Steven A., Brief History of the Ground fish Industry in New England, www.nefsc.noaa.

Statement on Signing the Fishery Conservation and Management Act, President Gerald R. Ford, The White House, April 13, 1976.

President Harry S. Truman, Proclamation 2668, September 28, 1945.

Hemingway, Ernest, The Old Man and the Sea, *Scribner*, 1952.

President Harry S. Truman, Proclamation 2667, September 28, 1945.

King, Rob, Sinking Fast: How Factory Trawlers are Destroying U.S. Fisheries, 1976.

Bailey, Kevin, Billion Dollar Fish: The Untold Story of Alaska Pollock, *University of Chicago Press Books*, 2013.

The Postwar Expansion of Russia's Fishing Industry, Fisheries Research Institute, University of Washington, January 1964.

Woodford, Riley, No One in Alaska died in Commercial Fishing in the Past Year, *Alaska Fish and Wildlife News*, January 2016.

Sanford, William F. Jr., The Marshall Plan: Origins and Implementation, U.S. Department of State, June 1982.

Chapter 4: Alaska's Lands

Hopkins, Regina Marie, The Alaska National Monuments of 1978: Another Chapter in the Great Alaskan Land War, *Boston College Environmental Affairs Law Review,* 1979, Volume 8, Issue 1.

Turner, Wallace, Areas as Vast as whole states now change hands in Alaska, *New York Times*, October 8, 1982.

Linxwiler, James D., The Alaska Native Claims Settlement Act at 35, Delivering on the Promises, *Guess and Rudd*, 2007.

Claims Bill Sails Through, *Tundra Ties,* December 18, 1971.

Thomas, Monica E., The Alaska Native Claims Settlement Act: Conflict and Controversy, *Polar Record,* April 1985.

Federal Land Ownership by State, https://ballotpedia.org.

Public Law 92-203, December 18, 1971.

Modern Alaska, http://www.akhistorycourse.org.

History of the Public Lands in Alaska, https://AlaskaCenters.gov.

Designation of National Monuments in Alaska, Statement by President Jimmy Carter, The White House, December 1, 1978, www.Presidency.ucsb.edu.

American Antiquities Act of 1906, 16 U.S.C. 431-433.

Hearing by the Committee on Merchant Marine and Fisheries Subcommittee on Fisheries Conservation and the Environment, University of Alaska at Fairbanks, March 10, 1979, Serial No. 96.5.

Report of the Committee on Interior and Insular Affairs on H.R. 39, Alaska Interest Lands Conservation Act, House Report 96-97, Part I, April 18, 1979.

Report of the Committee on Merchant Marine and Fisheries on H.R. 39, Alaska Interest Lands Conservation Act, House Report 96-97, Part II, April 23, 1979.

Statement by Congressman Morris K. Udall on the floor of the House of Representatives, Concerning H.R. 39, *Congressional Record,* May 16, 1979, Page H11454.

Statement by Congressman Don Young on the floor of the House of Representatives, Concerning H.R. 39, *Congressional Record,* May 16, 1979, Page H12690.

Statement by Congressman John Dingell, on the floor of the House of Representatives, Concerning H.R. 39,

Congressional Record, May 16, 1979, Page H11360.

Statement by Congressman Don Young on the floor of the House of Representatives, Concerning H.R. 39, *Congressional Record,* May 16, 1979, Page H13364.

Report of the Senate Committee on Energy and Natural Resources on H.R. 39, November 14, 1979, Senate Report 96-413, Page 433.

Statement by Congressman Don Young on the floor of the House or Representatives Concerning H.R. 39, *Congressional Record,* November 12, 1980, Page H10530.

Toddernd, Eric, The Alaska Lands Act: A Delicate Balance between Conservation and Development, *Public Lands and Resources Law Review* Volume 8, 1987.

Secretary Hodel Says Oil and Gas Leasing on the Coastal Plain would be consistent with protection of wildlife at Arctic National Wildlife Refuge, Department of the Interior, April 20, 1987.

Collins, Keith, Obama has Established more National Monuments than any other President, January 12, 2017.

Chapter 5: Historic Election

Historical Information of the Committee on Resources and its Predecessor Committees, 1807-2002, Committee on

Resources, Committee Print 107-G, November 2002.

The Treasure of the Sierra Madre, Quotes, IMDb, www.imdb.com/title.

Burger, Timothy J. and Jacoby, Mary, Republicans Sworn in to 104th Congress as Hill's New Power Rangers, *Roll Call,* January 5, 1995, Pages 1 and 15.

Chapter 6: Chairman of Resources

Fishery Conservation and Management Amendments of 1995, Committee on Resources, June 30, 1995, Rept. 104-171.

Statement by Congressman Don Young on the floor of the House of Representatives Concerning H.R. 39, Fishery Conservation and Management Amendments of 1995, *Congressional Record,* September 18, 1995, Page H9117.

Statement by Congressman Gerry Studds on the floor of the House of Representatives Concerning H.R. 39, *Congressional Record,* September 18, 1995, Page H9188.

Statement by Congressman Don Young on the floor of the House of Representatives Concerning H.R. 39, *Congressional Record,* September 18, 1995, Page H11436.

Statement on the Signing of the Sustainable Fisheries Act, The White House, October 11, 1996.

The Economic Value of Alaska's Seafood Industry, Alaska Seafood Marketing Institute, McDowell Group, December 2015.

Current Fishery Statistics, NOAA Fisheries, Imports and Exports of Fishery Products, Annual Summary, 2015.

Statement by Congressman Gerry Studds on the floor of the House of Representatives Concerning S. 39, Sustainable Fisheries Act, *Congressional Record,* September 27, 1996, Page H11439.

Statement by Congressman Don Young on the floor of the House of Representatives Concerning H.R. 1675, National Wildlife Refuge System Improvement Act, *Congressional Record,* May 18, 1995, Page H5358.

Secretary Bruce Babbitt Outlines Principles, Directives for National Wildlife Refuges. Withdraws Support of Legislation, *U.S. Fish and Wildlife Service News,* December 15, 1995.

Statement by Congressman Don Young on the floor of the House of Representatives Concerning H.R. 1675, *Congressional Record,* April 24, 1996, Page H3375.

Statement by Congressman Don Young at the Subcommittee on Fisheries Conservation, Wildlife, and Oceans Hearing on H.R. 511, National Wildlife

Refuge System Improvement Act of 1997, March 6, 1997, Page 3, Serial Number 105-7.

Statement by Congressman Don Young on the floor of the House of Representatives Concerning H.R. 511, *Congressional Record,* February 6, 1997, Page 15181.

Letter to Chairman Young from Secretary of the Interior, Bruce Babbitt, April 29, 1997.

Statement by Congressman Don Young on the floor of the House of Representatives Concerning H.R. 1420, National Wildlife Refuge System Improvement Act, June 3, 1997, Page H3227.

Statement by Congressman John Dingell on the floor of the House of Representatives Concerning H.R. 1420, National Wildlife Refuge System Improvement Act, *Congressional Record,* June 3, 1997, Page H3229.

Statement by Congressman George Miller on the floor of the House of Representatives Concerning H.R. 1420, National Wildlife Refuge System Improvement Act, *Congressional Record,* June 3, 1997, Page H3229.

Statement by Congressman Ron Paul on the floor of the House of Representatives Concerning H.R. 1420, National Wildlife Refuge System Improvement Act,

Congressional Record, June 3, 1997, Page H3232.

Letter to the Honorable Trent Lott from Congressmen Don Young and Jim Saxton, June 9, 1997.

Statement by Congressman Don Young on the floor of the House of Representatives Concerning H.R. 1420, National Wildlife Refuge System Improvement Act, *Congressional Record*, September 23, 1997, Page H7647.

Memorandum for the President from Bruce Babbitt, Secretary of the Interior, National Wildlife Legislation, July 23, 1997.

Statement on the Signing of the National Wildlife Refuge System Improvement act of 1997, The White House, October 9, 1997.

Statement by Congressman Don Young on the floor of the House of Representatives Concerning H.R. 2863, Migratory Bird Treaty Reform Act. *Congressional Record,* February 12, 1997, Page E245.

Statement of William P. Horn at the Subcommittee on Fisheries Conservation, Wildlife, and Oceans Hearing on H.R. 2863, May 15, 1997, Page 30, Serial Number 105-23.

Statement of Bill Boe at the Subcommittee on Fisheries Conservation, Wildlife, and

Oceans Hearing on H.R. 2863, May 15, 1997, Page 44, Serial Number 105-23.

Statement of Congressman Don Young on the floor of the House of Representatives Concerning H.R. 2863, *Congressional Record*, November 6, 1997, Page E2208.

Report from the Committee on Environment and Public Works on H.R. 2863, October 5,1998, Report 105-366.

Statement of Congressman Don Young on the floor of the House of Representatives Concerning H.R. 2863, *Congressional Record*, September 10, 1998, Page H7504.

Letter of Larry D. Closson, Chief, Office of Law Enforcement, Illinois Department of Natural Resources concerning H.R. 2863, *Congressional Record*, September 10, 1998, Page H7502.

Statement on the signing of the Wildlife and Wetlands legislation, The White House, October 30, 1998.

Chapter 7: Chairman of Transportation

Report of the Select Committee on Homeland Security, Homeland Security Act of 2002, July 24, 2002, House Report 107-609, Part 1.

Statement by Congressman Dick Armey on the floor of the House of Representatives Concerning H.R. 5005, Homeland Security Act of 2002,

Congressional Record, July 25, 2002, Page H5634.

Statement by Congressman Don Young on the floor of the House of Representatives Concerning H.R. 5005, Homeland Security Act of 2002, *Congressional Record,* July 25, 2002, Page H5687.

Statement of President George W. Bush on the signing of the Homeland Security Act, The White House, November 25, 2002.

Summary of Legislative and Oversight Activities, Committee on Transportation and Infrastructure, December 20, 2002, House Report 107-793.

Who Joined HHS, U.S. Department of Homeland Security, September 15 2015, www.dhs.gov.

Statement of Congressman John Mica on the floor of the House of Representatives Concerning H.R. 2215, Vision 100: A Century of Aviation Reauthorization Act, *Congressional Record,* June 11, 2003, Page H5202.

Report of the Committee on Transportation and Infrastructure on H.R. 2215, June 6, 2003, Page 49.

Statement of Congressman Don Young on the floor of the House of Representatives Concerning H.R. 2215, *Congressional Record,* June 11, 2003, Page H5201.

Statement of Congressman James Oberstar on the floor of the House of Representatives Concerning H.R. 2215, *Congressional Record,* June 11, 2003, Page H5201.

Statement of Congressman Don Young on the floor of the House of Representatives Concerning H.R. 2215, *Congressional Record,* June 11, 2003, Page H5236.

Statement of Congressman Don Young on the floor of the House of Representatives Concerning H.R. 2215, *Congressional Record,* October 30, 2003, Page H10178.

Signing Statement of President George W. Bush, The White House, H.R. 2215, December 12, 2003.

Aircraft Owners and Pilots Association Pays Tribute to Alaska's Rep. Don Young with Prestigious Hartranet Award, November 11, 2009.

Hall, Anthony F., Nixon's Speech at the Sagamore was birthplace of Interstate Highway System, *Lake George Mirror Magazine,* January 20, 2011.

Statement by President Dwight D. Eisenhower, The White House, To the Congress of the United States, February 27, 1955.
Statement of Congressman Don Young on the floor of the House of Representatives Concerning H.R 3, SAFETEA-LU,

351

Congressional Record, February 14, 2005, Page E226.

Statement of Congressman Don Young on the floor of the House of Representatives Concerning H.R 3, SAFETEA-LU, *Congressional Record,* March 9, 2005, Page H1038.

Statement of Congressman James Oberstar on the floor of the House of Representatives Concerning H.R 3, SAFETEA-LU, *Congressional Record,* March 9, 2005, Page H1041.

Statement of Congressman Hal Rogers on the floor of the House of Representatives Concerning H.R 3, SAFETEA-LU, *Congressional Record,* March 9, 2005, Page H1053.

Statement of Congressman Jimmy Duncan on the floor of the House of Representatives Concerning H.R 3, SAFETEA-LU, *Congressional Record,* March 9, 2005, Page H1053.

Statement of Congresswoman Eleanor Holmes Norton on the floor of the House of Representatives Concerning H.R 3, SAFETEA-LU, *Congressional Record,* March 9, 2005, Page H1049.

Statement of Congressman Peter DeFazio on the floor of the House of Representatives Concerning H.R 3, SAFETEA-LU, *Congressional Record,* March 9, 2005, Page H1039.

Statement of Congressman Don Young on the floor of the House of Representatives Concerning H.R 3, SAFETEA-LU, *Congressional Record,* July 29, 2005, Page H7571

Statement on the Signing of H.R. 3, Safe, Accountable, Flexible, Efficient Transportation Equity Act: A Legacy for Users, The White House, August 10, 2005.

Federal Highway Administration: A Summary of Highway Provisions in SAFETEA-LU, August 25, 2005.

Chapter 8: Dean of the House

Medeiros, Andrea, U.S. Fish and Wildlife Service Published Final Rule for Alaska's National Wildlife Refuges Non-Subsistence Take of Wildlife and Closure Regulations, January 13, 2016.

State of Alaska v Sally Jewell, United States District Court for the District of Alaska, January 13, 2017.

Statement by Congressman Don Young on the floor of the House of Representatives Concerning H. J. Res, 69, Wildlife Refuges Disapproval Resolution, *Congressional Record,* February 16, 2017, Page H1260.

Statement by Senator Lisa Murkowski on the floor of the U.S. Senate Concerning H.

J. Res. 69, *Congressional Record,* March 21, 2017,
Page S. 1867.

President Donald J. Trump signs Resolution Overturning U.S. Fish and Wildlife Service's Regulations, Press Release of Congressman Don Young, April 4, 2017.

Eilperin, Juliet, Senate Votes to Kill Rule on Hunting in Alaska, *Washington Post,* March 23, 2017.

Secretary of Interior Sally Jewell Issues decision on Izembek National Wildlife Refuge Land Exchange and Road Proposal, December 23, 2013.

Testimony of Della Trumble, Lifelong Aleut Resident of King Cove and Community Spokesperson, at the House Natural Resources Subcommittee on Federal Lands Concerning H.R. 218, King Cove Land Exchange Act, April 5, 2017.

Statement of Congressman Don Young on the floor of the House of Representatives Concerning H.R. 218, *Congressional Record,* July 20, 2017, Pages H6120-6121.

Congressman Young leads House passage of King Cove Land Exchange Act, July 20, 2017.

United States Department of the Department of the Interior, U.S Fish and Fish and Wildlife Service, January 22, 2018.

Secretary Zinke Approves Initial Plan to Build a Life-Saving Road for Alaska Native Village of King Cove, U. S. Department of the Interior, Press Release, January 22, 2018.

Alaska Delegation Hails Landmark Agreement for Life-Saving Road, Press Release of Congressman Don Young, January 22, 2018.

House Report 115-154, to Authorize the Expansion of an existing Hydroelectric Project, Committee on Natural Resources, June 2, 2017.

Statement of Congressman Don Young on the floor of the House of Representatives Concerning H.R. 220, Terror Lake Hydroelectric Project, *Congressional Record,* June 27, 2017, Page H5204.

Indian Energy Development: Poor management by BIA has hindered energy development on Indian lands, U.S. Government Accountability Office, June 15, 2015.

Young's Native American Energy Act Approved in Committee, Press Release of Congressman Don Young, October 4, 2017.

Chapter 9: ANWR

The Inupiat Eskimo of Kaktovik, Alaska, Cultural History, http://arcticcircle.unconn.edu.

Public Land Order 2214, U.S. Fish and Wildlife Service, www.fws.gov.

Public Law 96-487.

Statement by Senator Paul Tsongas on the floor of the U.S. Senate Concerning H.R. 39, Alaska Interest Lands Conservation Act, *Congressional Record,* August 18, 1980, Page S21656.

Secretary Don Hodel says Oil and Gas Leasing on Coastal Plain would be consistent with protection of wildlife at Arctic National Wildlife Refuge, *Department of the Interior News Release,* April 20, 1987.

Hearing on Arctic National Wildlife Refuge, Subcommittee on Fisheries and Wildlife Conservation and the Environment, March 31, 1988, Page 481.

Arctic Coastal Plain Competitive Oil and Gas Leasing Act, Senate Committee on Energy and Natural Resources, March 24, 1988, Senate Report 100-308.

Statement by Congressman Don Young on the floor of the House of Representatives Concerning H.R. 4, Energy Policy Act, *Congressional Record,* August 1, 2001, Page H5160.

Statement by Congressman Don Young on the floor of the House of Representatives Concerning H.R. 6, Energy Policy Act,

Congressional Record, April 11, 2003, Page H3251.

Statement by Congressman Don Young on the floor of the House of Representatives Concerning H.R. 3408, Pioneers Act, *Congressional*, February 15, 2012, Page H753.

Statement by Congressman Billy Tauzin on the floor of the House of Representatives Concerning H.R. 4, Energy Policy Act, *Congressional Record,* August 1, 2001, Page H5161.

Corn, M. Lynne, Arctic National Wildlife Refuge Votes and Legislative Actions Since the 95ᵗʰ Congress, *Congressional Research Service,* December 14, 2016.

Secretarial Order 3352, United State Department of the Interior, May 31, 2017.

Statement by Congressman Don Young on the floor of the House of Representatives Concerning H. Con. Res. 71, *Congressional Record,* October 4, 2017, Page H7792.

Statement by Senator Lisa Murkowski at the Senate Energy and Natural Resources Committee Hearing on Opening the 1002 Area to Responsible Development, November 2, 2017.

Statement by Congressman Don Young at the Senate Energy and Natural Resources Committee Hearing on Opening the 1002

Area to Responsible Development, November 2, 2017.

Statement by Alaska Lieutenant Governor Byron Mallot at the Senate Energy and Natural Resources Committee Hearing on Opening the 1002 Area to Responsible Development, November 2, 2017.

Statement by Matthew Rexford, Tribal Administrator, Native Village of Kaktovik at the Senate Energy and Natural Resources Committee Hearing on Opening the 1002 Area to Responsible Development, November 2, 2017.

Statement by Speaker of the House Paul Ryan on the floor of the House of Representatives Concerning H.R. 1, The Tax Cuts and Jobs Act, *Congressional Record,* December 19, 2017, Page H10212.

Statement by President Donald J. Trump, The White House, December 22, 2017.

www.DonYoung.gov.

Chapter 10: Final Reflections

Jenkins, Paul, Even Young's Enemies Know he has produced for Alaska, *The Anchorage Times,* April 24, 2008.

Martinson, Eric, "Why Quit? Rep. Don Young, 85 and proud of his accomplishments, says he has energy for a 24th term," Anchorage Daily News, June 7, 2018.

Stanton, John, Colleagues Mourn the Death of Stevens, *Roll Call,* August 10, 2010.

Statement by the Speaker of the House Paul Ryan on the floor of the House of Representatives Honoring Don Young as Dean of the House of Representatives, *Congressional Record,* January 10, 2018, Page H 112.

Statement by Congressman Nancy Pelosi on the floor of the House of Representatives Honoring Don Young as Dean of the House of Representatives, *Congressional Record,* January 10, 2018, Page H 112.

Statement by Congressman Don Young on the floor of the House of Representatives Honoring Don Young as Dean of the House of Representatives, *Congressional Record,* January 10, 2018, Pages H 112-113.

The Reliable Source, *The Washington Post,* June 10, 2015.

Whitney, David, Young Lifts No. 39 to Tweak Old Foes, *Anchorage Daily News,* January 16, 1997.

Gayle and Harry Burroughs in
Seward, Alaska.

Harry Frederick Burroughs III was born in
Riverhead, New York. He began his career
in the U.S. House of Representatives on
May 16, 1977. For the next thirty-seven
years, he worked for six members of
Congress, served as Republican Chief of
Staff of the House Merchant Marine and
Fisheries Committee, and Staff Director of
the House Natural Resources
Subcommittee on Fisheries, Wildlife,
Oceans, and Insular Affairs.

In 1985, Harry first met the Congressman for All of Alaska, Don Young. Over the next 30 years, he had a front row seat watching how the gentleman from Fort Yukon, Alaska became the longest serving Member of Congress from Alaska, the Dean of the House of Representatives, and one of the legislative giants in the history of the House of Representatives. This book is a long overdue tribute to this extraordinary man who passionately cares for and fights for all of his constituents who live in the great State of Alaska every day.

Since retiring from the House of Representatives in January 2015, Harry has written *My Life on Capitol Hill: Five Decades Working in the People's House*, *The National Wildlife Refuge System: History, Laws, and Abuses of Power*, and *The People's Sheriff which is a comprehensive analysis of the remarkably successful campaign waged by his friend Robert P. Mosier to become* the 60th Sheriff in Fauquier County Virginia history.

He lives with his wife, Gayle, in Warrenton, Virginia and they are blessed with four beautiful grandchildren Mitchell, Elise, Kelly, and Christopher.

Made in the USA
Middletown, DE
22 August 2019